SPECTRUM

6

A Communicative Course in English

Sandra Costinett
with Donald R. H. Byrd

Donald R. H. Byrd *Project Director*

Anna Veltfort *Art Director*

Education Curriculum

Prentice Hall Regents
Englewood Cliffs, NJ 07632

Library of Congress has cataloged this title as follows:
Costinett, Sandra.
 Spectrum 6: a communicative course in English / Sandra Costinett,
with Donald R.H. Byrd; Donald R.H. Byrd, project director; Anna
Veltfort, art director.
  p. cm.
 ISBN 0-13-830233-2
 1. English language—Textbooks for foreign speakers. I. Byrd,
Donald R.H. II. Title. III. Title: Spectrum six.
PE1128.C726 1994   94-5461
428.2'4—dc20   CIP

Project Manager: Nancy L. Leonhardt
Manager of Development Services: Louisa B. Hellegers
Editorial Consultant: Larry Anger
Contributing Writer: Gerry Strei
Development Editor: Stephanie Karras
Audio Development Editor: D. Andrew Gitzy
Assistant to the Editors: Jennifer Fader
Reading Researchers and Writers: Sylvia P. Bloch, Randee Falk, Virginia Lowe
Director of Production and Manufacturing: David Riccardi
Editorial Production/Design Manager: Dominick Mosco
Production Editor and Compositor: Christine McLaughlin Mann
Page Composition: Ken Liao, Steve Jorgensen
Electronic Production Coordinator: Molly Pike Riccardi
Production Coordinator: Ray Keating
Production Assistant: Wanda España

Cover Design Coordinator: Merle Krumper
Cover Design: Roberto de Vicq
Electronic Art: Todd Ware, Rolando Corujo

Interior Concept and Page-by-Page Design: Anna Veltfort

© 1994 by PRENTICE HALL REGENTS
Prentice Hall, Inc.
A Paramount Communications Company
Englewood Cliffs, NJ 07632

Printed in the United States of America

10 9 8 7 6 5 4 3 2 1

ISBN 0-13-830233-2

Prentice Hall International (UK) Limited, London
Prentice Hall of Australia Pty. Limited, Sydney
Prentice Hall Canada, Inc., Toronto
Prentice Hall Hispanoamericana, S.A., Mexico
Prentice Hall of India Private Limited, New Delhi
Prentice Hall of Japan, Inc., Tokyo
Simon & Schuster Asia Pte. Ltd., Singapore
Editora Prentice Hall do Brasil, Ltda., Rio de Janeiro

Printed on Recycled Paper

REVIEWERS AND CONSULTANTS

For the preparation of the new edition, Prentice Hall Regents would like to thank the following long-time users of
Spectrum, whose insights and suggestions have helped to shape the content and format of the new edition: Motofumi
Aramaki, Sony Language Laboratory, Tokyo, Japan; Associacão Cultural Brasil-Estados Unidos (ACBEU), Salvador-
Bahia, Brazil; AUA Language Center, Bangkok, Thailand, Thomas J. Kral and faculty; Pedro I. Cohen, Professor
Emeritus of English, Linguistics, and Education, Universidad de Panamá; ELSI Taiwan Language Schools, Taipei,
Taiwan, Kenneth Hou and faculty; James Hale, Sundai ELS, Tokyo, Japan; Impact, Santiago, Chile; Instituto Brasil-
Estados Unidos (IBEU), Rio de Janeiro, Brazil; Instituto Brasil-Estados Unidos No Ceará (IBEU-CE), Fortaleza,
Brazil; Instituto Chileno Norteamericano de Cultura, Santiago, Chile; Instituto Cultural Argentino Norteamericano
(ICANA), Buenos Aires, Argentina; Christopher M. Knott, Chris English Masters Schools, Kyoto, Japan; The Language
Training and Testing Center, Taipei, Taiwan, Anthony Y. T. Wu and faculty; Lutheran Language Institute, Tokyo,
Japan; Network Cultura, Ensino e Livraria Ltda, São Paulo, Brazil; Seven Language and Culture, São Paulo, Brazil.

SPECIAL ACKNOWLEDGMENTS FOR LEVEL 6

Kevin McClure, ELS, San Francisco, CA; Elise Klein, ELS, New Haven, CT; Monica Haupt, ELS, Oakland, CA;
Maureen Daly of New Haven, CT.

INTRODUCTION

Welcome to the new edition of *Spectrum*! *Spectrum 6* represents the sixth level of a six-level course designed for adolescent and adult learners of English. The student book, workbook, and audio program for each level provide practice in all four communication skills, with a special focus on listening and speaking. Levels 1 and 2 are appropriate for beginning students and "false" beginners. Levels 3 and 4 are intended for intermediate classes, and 5 and 6 for advanced learners of English. The first four levels are offered in split editions—1A, 1B, 2A, 2B, 3A, 3B, 4A, and 4B. The student books, workbooks, audio programs, and teacher's editions for levels 1 to 4 are also available in full editions.

Spectrum is a "communicative" course in English, based on the idea that communication is not merely an end-product of language study, but rather the very process through which a new language is acquired. *Spectrum* involves students in this process from the very beginning by providing them with useful, natural English along with opportunities to discuss topics of personal interest and to communicate their own thoughts, feelings, and ideas.

In *Spectrum*, comprehension is considered the starting point for communication. The student books thus emphasize the importance of comprehension, both as a useful skill and as a natural means of acquiring a language. Throughout the unit students encounter readings and dialogues containing structures and expressions not formally introduced until later units or levels. The goal is to provide students with a continuous stream of input that challenges their current knowledge of English, thereby allowing them to progress naturally to a higher level of competence.

Spectrum emphasizes interaction as another vital step in language acquisition. Interaction begins with simple communication tasks that motivate students to use the same structure a number of times as they exchange real information about themselves and other topics. This focused practice builds confidence and fluency and prepares students for more open-ended activities involving role playing, discussion, and problem solving. These activities give students control of the interaction and enable them to develop strategies for expressing themselves and negotiating meaning in an English-speaking environment.

The *Spectrum* syllabus is organized around functions and structures practiced in thematic lessons. Both functions and structures are carefully graded according to level of difficulty and usefulness. Structures are presented in clear paradigms with informative usage notes. Thematic lessons provide interesting topics for interaction and a meaningful vehicle for introducing vocabulary.

This student book consists of twelve units. Each unit begins with a preview page that outlines the functions/themes, language, and forms (grammar) in the unit. Preview activities prepare students to understand the content of the readings that begin each unit and give them the opportunity to draw upon their own background knowledge. The first lesson in each unit establishes the theme with a reading selection. Students read authentic newspaper or magazine articles that have been carefully adapted for use in *Spectrum*. The articles are accompanied by a variety of as-you-read and follow-up activities that develop reading skills. The next lesson presents a realistic conversation, providing input for comprehension and language acquisition. New functions and structures are then practiced through interactive tasks in a three-page thematic lesson. The next two-page lesson includes discussion or role-playing activities that draw on students' personal experience, and a listening exercise related to the theme of the unit. The final lesson of the unit presents a variety of situations, photos, artwork, short articles, or listening passages as springboards for writing practice. There are review lessons after units 6 and 12. An accompanying workbook, audio cassette program, and teacher's edition are available.

S C O P E   A N D

SEQUENCE

LANGUAGE	FORMS	SKILLS
Who's the woman (who's) drinking coffee? That's Olga Sandoval. Do you know what *budín de tortilla* is? It's a casserole made with tortillas, chicken, and cheese. I've never seen *Citizen Kane*. What's it about? It's a story modeled on the life of the famous newspaper publisher, William Randolph Hearst. My teacher used to sit at her desk the whole day, waiting for us to do something wrong. He sat in his room all morning playing the guitar. She banged on the wall loudly, making a lot of noise.	Relative clauses with pronouns as subjects: Reduced restrictive clauses Placement of adverbs	Listen to recollections of the past Write a newspaper review
There's a computer technology conference that I would like to attend. It's a very important meeting and I think it's essential that I go. It is essential for us to fill the vacancy left by Mr. Franco. Karen just bought a new television and a stereo and now she wants a personal computer. You know what they say: The more you get, the more you want. Speed limits have a purpose, and the sooner you start paying attention to them, the better for everyone. Larry, could you help me for a minute, please? Melissa, I'd like you to help me for a minute, please.	Subjunctive clauses vs. infinitive clauses Double comparatives	Listen to people make judgments Write a memo
What are your plans for the future? After I graduate, I'll get a job and work for five or ten years. By then, I will have gotten some experience. I've decided to quit my job. By the end of this year, I will have been working for the company for four years, and I haven't even had a promotion yet. Futurist Ronald Herd feels that dwellings will have changed significantly by the year 2025. What do you suppose your life would be like if you hadn't finished high school? Well, I suppose I'd be working in a boring job somewhere, and I probably wouldn't speak a word of English. Whenever I talk to Chris, he laughs, even when we're talking about something serious. I'm sure if he weren't so nervous, he wouldn't laugh all the time.	The future perfect and the future perfect continuous Mixed contrary-to-fact conditional sentences: Present and past	Listen to someone talk about his life Write an answer a letter
What do you think of Leslie? I think she's nice, and I appreciate her always being so frank. But I'm getting tired of her teasing me about my diet. I just can't stand being talked about behind my back. I don't like to be talked about either. Not only don't you help me around the house, but you also don't help me with the kids. I'm tired of your assuming that I'll do everything. The Wakefield Little Theater either wants to lose money, or it has the worst luck in the history of local theater groups.	Infinitives with subjects vs. gerunds with subjects *Either . . . or*, *neither . . . nor*, and *not only . . . but (also)*	Write a letter of complaint Listen to someone talk about his feelings
You know, I tried to get hold of Mike all weekend, but the phone was always busy. He couldn't have been talking that whole time. Maybe the phone was off the hook. I suppose it might have been. We're looking for a red-haired woman who stole a white Toyota. Did you happen to see her? I don't believe so. But I did see a gray-haired woman riding a bike and holding a cat under her arm, which I thought was odd. The woman we're looking for, who we think had on a black skirt, was very tall and she was wearing glasses. The Freeman Gallery, which is located in London, sells paintings and other art objects. It seems to me that they must have climbed in through the window.	Short answers with modal auxiliaries Nonrestrictive vs. restrictive relative clauses	Listen to people speculate about possibilities Write a police report
Do you like modern dance? Actually, I'm not all that crazy about it. What I really like is folk dancing. There's a new exhibit of fifteenth-century Italian paintings at the museum. Maybe we ought to go there sometime. That might be interesting, but modern art is what I really like. That sounds good, but what I'd really like to see sometime is an opera. There's nothing wrong with innovative styles, yet I'm personally more comfortable with a conservative look. Well, you might like it once you get used to it. I love opera, whereas my husband can't stand it. He said he'd rather listen to a cat fight. How did you react when he said that? I just laughed it off.	Special word order for emphasis Connectors *in spite of* and *despite*; *yet*; *nevertheless* and *nonetheless*; *whereas* and *while*; and *however* and *on the other hand*	Listen for tactful or tactless responses Write a letter
Review	Review	Review

ACKNOWLEDGMENTS

ILLUSTRATIONS

Pages 62, 73, 110, 111, 116, 117, and 136 by Anna Veltfort; pages 14, 21, 36, 37, 44, 80, 81, 98, 112, and 113 by Anne Burgess; pages 32, 33, 45, and 46 by Hugh Harrison; pages 4, 5, 10, 24, 54, 89, 92, 99, and 118 by Randy Jones; pages 58, 59, 96, and 97 by Eileen McKeating; pages 7, 20, 31, 34, 51, 52, 60, 64, 66, 72, 79, 102, 106, 107, 124, 128, and 132 by V. Gene Myers; pages 69, 70, and 109 by Charles Peale; pages 30, 35, 38, 39, 50, 82, 94, 122, 126, and 127 by Bot Roda; pages 25, 26, 40, 55, 56, 75, 84, 85, 93, and 95 by Arnie Ten.

PHOTOS

Page 1 by Photofest; page 2 by NASA; page 9 by Bill Anderson/Monkmeyer Press; page 11 by Reuters/Bettmann; pages 12, 13 (bottom) and 100 by UPI/Bettmann; pages 13 (top) and 121 by AP/Wide World Photos; page 18 (top) by Donna Jernigan; page 18 (middle) by Daemrich/The Image Works; page 18 (bottom) by Michael Newman/Photo Edit; pages 19 and 78 (middle right) by Bill Bachmann/Photo Researchers, Inc.; page 22 by Jerome Wexler/FPG International; page 23 (top) by Beryl Goldberg/Monkmeyer Press; page 23 (bottom) by Howard Dratch/The Image Works; pages 28 and 29 (top left) by Porterfield/Chickering/Photo Researchers; page 29 (top right) by Hugh Rogers/Monkmeyer Press; pages 29 (bottom left), 77 (middle), and 104 (box 3) by Chester Higgins, Jr./Photo Researchers, Inc.; page 29 (bottom right) by Ken Ross/FPG; pages 41(left), 49(top), and 120 (left) by Bettman Archives; page 41 (right) by Victor Englebert/ Photo Researchers, Inc.; page 42 (top) by Louise L. Serpa/Photo Researchers, Inc.; page 42 (middle) by Kenneth Murray/Photo Researchers, Inc.; page 42 (bottom) by Mark Antman/The Image Works; page 48 (top) by Collections of the Library of Congress; page 48 (bottom) by Arlene Collins/Monkmeyer Press Photo Service; page 49 (middle) by The Makers of Armstrong's Linoleum; page 49 (bottom) by Maria Pape; page 65 by Mark Lennihan; page 71 by *Xplora 1: Peter Gabriel's Secret World* ©1993 Real World Multi Media Ltd.; page 76 (top left) by Mark Humphrey/AP Photo; page 76 (top right) by Jacksonville Symphony Association; page 76 (bottom left) by Sergio Penchansky/Photo Researchers Inc.; page 76 (bottom right) by Randy Matusow/Monkmeyer Press; page 77 (top) by Star File; page 77 (bottom) by Mimi Forsyth/Monkmeyer Press; page 78 (top left) by David Powers; page 78 (top right) by Carol Rosegg/Martha Swope Associates; page 78 (middle left) by Boris Erwitt/FPG International; page 78 (bottom left) by John Moore Photography; page 78 (bottom right) by Joel Gordon Photography; page 86 (top left) by Ann Holmes/Photo Researchers, Inc.; page 86 (top right) by Dick Davis/Photo Researchers, Inc.; page 86 (bottom left) by George Holton/Photo Researchers, Inc.; page 86 (bottom right) by F. Sacristan/Gamma-Liaison, Inc.; page 87 by R. Matusow/Monkmeyer Press; pages 90 and 91 by Frank LaBua; page 101 (top) by Gamma; page 101 (bottom) by NBT; page 104 (box 1) by Rhoda Sidney/ Monkmeyer Press; page 104 (box 2) by A. Albert/The Image Works; page 104 (box 4) by Peter Menzel/Stock Boston, Inc.; page 104 (box 5) by Doug Plummer/Photo Rearchers, Inc.; page 119 (top left) by Spencer Grant/ Monkmeyer Press; page 119 (top right) by Jay Berndt/Stock Boston, Inc.; page 119 (bottom left) by Michael Kagan/ Monkmeyer Press; page 119 (bottom right) by Roberta Hershenson/Photo Researchers, Inc.; page 120 (right) by Martha Swope Assoc.

REALIA

Pages 3, 5, 6, 8, 9, 15, 16, 17, 33, 42, 43, 45, 47 (top), 52-53, 57, 61, 63, 65, 67, 70, 71, 83, 84, 87, 88, 90, 94, 96, 108, 115, 118, 120, 125, 126, 127, 131, 133, 134, and 135 by Siren Design; pages 19, 26, 28, 29, 35, 36, 39, 47 (bottom), 50, 60, 62, 98, 104, 105, 128, and 129 by Anna Veltfort.

PERMISSIONS

Pages 12-13: ©1980 by The New York Times Company. Reprinted by permission. Pages 22-23: Reprinted by permission of *Psychology Today* magazine. ©1984, American Psychological Association. Page 32: ©1981 by The New York Times Company. Reprinted by permission. Pages 42-43: Written by Murray Rubenstein. Originally published by *Science Digest*. Page 52:©1984 by The New York Times Copmpany. Reprinted by permission. Page 61: Reprinted with permission of Science Digest, ©1985 by The Hearst Corporation. Page 67: Adapted with permission of Collier Associates from Unlocking Opportunity by Catherine Lilly and Daniel Martin, ©1985 by Catherine Lilly and Daniel Martin. Page 80: Reprinted with permission of *Working Woman* magazine, ©1985 Hal Publications, Inc. Page 90: Reprinted by permission of *The Futurist*, published by The World Future Society. Pages 100-101: Nuestro magazine, June/July 1982. Pages 110-111: WGBH-Boston, NOVA ©1985 Addison-Wesley, Reading, MA. Pages 120-121: ©1984 by The New York Times Company. Reprinted with permission. Page 129: Repritned with permission of *Psychology Today* magazine, ©1985 American Psychological Association. Page 131: Reprinted with permission of *Woman's World* magazine. Page 133: ©1985, USA TODAY. Reprinted with permission. Page 135: Reprinted with permission of *Psychology Today* magazine, ©1985 American Psychological Association.

The editors have made every effort to trace the ownership of all copyrighted material and express regret in advance for any error or omission. After notification of oversight, they will include proper acknowledgment in future printings.

FUNCTIONS/THEMES	LANGUAGE	FORMS
Debate an issue Support an argument	I'm against/in favor of teaching young children to cook. I agree/strongly disagree with that. A twelve-month school year is efficient. Furthermore, students won't forget what they've learned.	Conjunctions
Express regret Talk about hopes and wishes	I wish I'd learned to play a musical instrument when I was young. I hope I passed the test. I wish I'd passed the test.	*Hope* vs. *wish* in past time

Preview the reading.

1. Look at the photos below and discuss these questions in small groups: Have you ever seen any TV programs featuring the characters in the photos? If so, what is the name of the program? What is it about? If you're not familiar with the photos here, have you ever seen a movie or TV program about future life in outer space? What's your opinion about the possibility of such future life?

2. Before you read the article on page 2, look at the title and the pictures on pages 2–3. What do you think the article is about? Discuss your answer with a partner. Also discuss a possible answer to the question in the title.

1.

Space Stations:

Do they have a future?

Life on the space shuttle.

1 Many years from now, when people regularly take their vacations in outer space, they will look back on the twentieth century and try to date the beginning of the space age. Some will say it all started with the launching of Sputnik in 1957, others will point to Neil Armstrong's first steps on the moon in 1969, and still others will mention the birth of the space shuttle—a spacecraft that could be used more than once to make space travel much less expensive. But at least a few will emphasize that the true beginning was the creation of populated space stations.

2 A space station will actually be a home in space. It is designed so that many people can live and work for a longer time than they would be able to in an ordinary, crowded spacecraft. Through the doors of a space station, spacecraft will leave for the moon or even Mars at a fraction of the cost of launching them from Earth. In the space station's "rooms," astronauts and scientists will conduct important experiments in fields ranging from astronomy to chemistry.

3 The space station will have facilities for sleeping, bathing, exercising, eating, and relaxing. When it's time to sleep, astronauts will zip up in sleeping bags that hang from the wall. To shower in space, feet are strapped down, water is hosed on, and then the water is sucked up by a device like a vacuum cleaner. This water is then purified and recycled, as is the water for washing clothes. Astronauts will use a variety of exercise equipment to stay in shape, exercising about two hours a day. Food will be stored on the space station in one of two forms—dried or frozen. When astronauts want to eat, they will add liquid to dried food, or heat frozen food in a microwave oven. New supplies and fresh fruits and vegetables can be brought to the stations by shuttles. Astronauts will relax by watching videos, using the computer, reading, and talking to friends and family on Earth via radio.

4 Many experiments can be conducted on space station laboratories. Animals will be brought up into space to study the effects of weightlessness. Some will be living in the same conditions as the astronauts, while others will inhabit an area that is kept spinning to achieve a centrifugal force equal to Earth's gravity. These animals can then be studied to observe similarities and differences among the two groups in space and a control group on Earth. The lack of gravity in space also has benefits, mainly in the area of technology and manufacturing. Perhaps new alloys can be created from metals that do not mix on Earth. Computers and solar cells use crystals that could grow better in space. In the area of medicine, there is hope of new drugs being created that are purer and easier to manufacture.

5 And if space stations are successful, the next step may very well be space cities. Scientists believe that the benefits of space cities will far outweigh their costs. These space cities will help solve today's most pressing problems, among them overpopulation, the energy crisis, and pollution.

6 Not everyone agrees that we even need a space station, let alone space cities. Some scientists think that much experimentation and study must be done here on Earth before space stations are workable. They aren't sure that we should spend billions of dollars on a project whose technology is not yet established and whose benefits to the human race are still in question. These scientists think that the money could be better spent on shorter-range scientific research.

7 Nevertheless, an international partnership made up of the U.S., Japan, Canada, and ten European nations has been working on plans for Freedom—a space station designed both as a place for experimentation and research and as a spaceport for peopled trips to Mars. Begun in 1984, the program is struggling to continue despite criticism and budget cutbacks. Over the next few years, important decisions about the future of the Freedom space station, and the future of space exploration as a whole, will be made.

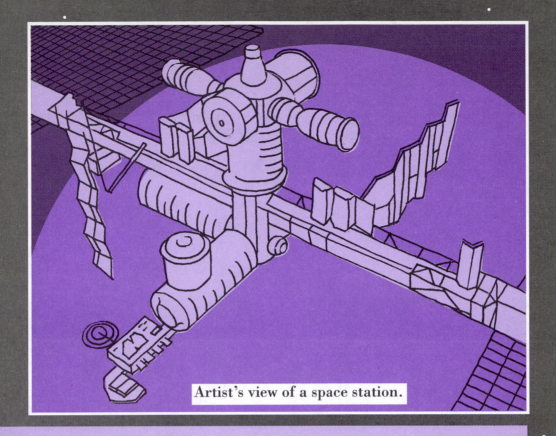

Artist's view of a space station.

Figure it out

1. Read the article. If necessary, change your answers to item 2 on page 1.

2. Look through the article for advantages and disadvantages of spending money on space stations. List the advantages and disadvantages. Then state whether the article argues more strongly for or against spending money on space stations.

3. Scan the article and find the paragraph that . . .

1. describes the facilities of space stations of the future.
2. discusses the early history of the space age.
3. discusses the plans for space cities.
4. describes experiments that will be carried out on space stations.
5. discusses plans for the Freedom space station.
6. gives reasons for opposing space stations.

4. Many words in English can be used as either nouns or verbs with no change in spelling or form. (In some cases, however, the stress or pronunciation may differ.) Find the words below in the article, and say if they are used as nouns or verbs. The words are listed in the order in which they appear.

1. date	8. study
2. travel	9. use
3. work	10. step
4. conduct	11. need
5. time	12. study
6. use	13. project
7. heat	

Compare:

Noun	*Verb*
cónduct	condúct
use [us]	use [uz]
próject	projéct

2. I don't agree...

1. Which of the following do you feel a country should spend the most money on? Rank the items in order of importance from 1 to 6. Then discuss your decision with a partner, giving arguments to support it.

_____ child care   _____ housing
_____ education   _____ scientific research
_____ health care   _____ space travel

 A group of college students is discussing the pros and cons of the space program.

Listen to the conversation.

---

(2)

Ramón We're here to discuss the space program. We have a limited amount of time, so let's get started.

Louisa I think the space program is a waste of money. Think of all the research scientists could be doing on disease with that money. Furthermore, the money is coming out of the taxpayers' pockets.

Ramón I'll admit that a lot has been spent on the program. However, I don't agree that the money has been wasted. The research they've done for the space program has brought all sorts of advances in other areas—in geology, medicine, manufacturing . . .

Keiko Not to mention all the new jobs the space program has created.

Louisa Well, I suppose some people have benefited from the program. Nevertheless, I still wish all this money had been put into something more useful—like cancer research, for instance.

Ramón But experiments involving medicine are being done on the space shuttle.

Keiko I think the space program is very useful and that someday we may be able to use the knowledge we've gained to live in outer space.

Andy Even if we understood perfectly how to live in outer space, the human race would never be able to survive there.

Ramón How can you be so sure of that? Not too long ago no one would have believed we could go to the moon.

Andy That may be, but the present is *here*, on Earth. Therefore, the money should be spent on problems the world faces right now.

Ramón Well, sorry, but that's all the time we have today. Let's continue our discussion tomorrow.

---

3. Find another way to say the words or expressions in italics.

1. The space program is a waste of money. *What's more*, taxpayers are paying for it.
2. The space program has been expensive. *But* it has advanced science and created jobs.
3. *Even so*, the money should have been spent on cancer research.
4. People don't live in space now. *So* we should spend our money here on Earth.

3. I disagree with that.

DEBATE AN ISSUE

1 ▶ Listen to the conversation.
▶ Act out similar conversations, using one of the opinions in the box or a different opinion. Use *what's more* or *besides* when you support an argument, *but* or *even so* when you counter an argument, and *so* when you draw a conclusion.

A I'm against teaching young children to cook. They usually make a mess and waste food.

B I agree. Besides, children can hurt themselves.

C Even so, I think children *should* learn how to cook. Everyone should learn to be self-sufficient.

D That's how I feel. Cooking isn't dangerous if children are taught safety rules.

E Well, I'm in favor of teaching girls to cook, but it's a waste of time to teach boys.

F I strongly disagree with that. Everyone eats, so everyone should know how to fix a meal.

Some opinions
Children should(n't) learn to cook.
Children should(n't) make their own decisions.
People should(n't) have to retire at a certain age.
Employees should(n't) call their bosses by their first names.
A person should(n't) get married before the age of thirty.

2 ▶ Read the Editorial and Editorial Rebuttal below. Then find a partner who agrees with you on one of the issues in the box. Work together and write a short editorial supporting your point of view.
▶ Exchange your editorial with a pair of students who took the other point of view, and write an answer to their editorial. Use some of the expressions in the box.

Are you for or against . . .
a twelve-month school year?
building more nuclear power plants?
spending more money on scientific research?
more child-care programs for working parents?
free university education for all students?
universal government-sponsored health coverage?

Some expressions	
First of all . . . Furthermore/Moreover . . .	◀ support an argument
But . . . However . . . Nevertheless . . .	◀ counter an argument
Therefore . . .	◀ draw a conclusion

Editorial

Time for a Twelve-Month School Year

The time has come to extend the school year to twelve months. If students attend school all year, they won't have the usual three months of summer vacation to forget what they've learned during the previous nine months. Moreover, there will be less risk of students' getting into trouble because they have too much unstructured time. Furthermore, a twelve-month school year will allow us to make full use of our public school facilities. We taxpayers should not have to pay for the upkeep of buildings that go unused for three months every year. Students may not like the idea of going to classes all year round. However, teachers and taxpayers will agree that it makes more sense than the traditional academic year.

– Alberto Campos

Editorial Rebuttal

Let's Keep the Nine-Month School Year

The twelve-month school year proposed by Alberto Campos in last week's paper may sound like a good idea to tired parents and dissatisfied taxpayers. Nevertheless, there are a lot of people who would be adversely affected by it. First of all, many students use the three months of summer vacation to earn the money they use to pay for books, clothing, and other necessary items during the school year. There are also many businesses whose customers are students on summer vacation. If the school year is extended to twelve months, summer camps for young people, like the one we operate, would be forced to close, and all of our employees would be out of work. The nine-month school year has worked well for a long time. Therefore, let's not try to fix what isn't broken.

– Carol and Roger Jenkins
Rolling Hills Summer Camp

3 ► **Study the frames: Conjunctions**

A twelve-month school year is efficient.	**What's more, Besides Furthermore, Moreover,**	students won't forget what they've learned.
A nine-month school year gives students longer vacations.	**However, Even so, Nevertheless,**	school buildings go unused for three months.
A nine-month school year gives students longer vacations,	**but**	school buildings go unused for three months.
A nine-month school year has worked well for a long time.	**Therefore,**	we should keep the traditional academic year.
A nine-month school year has worked well for a long time,	**so**	we should keep the traditional academic year.

Furthermore and *moreover* connect two ideas that support each other. These words mean *and*.

However and *nevertheless* connect ideas that counter each other. These words mean *but*.

Therefore introduces a logical conclusion.

In formal writing, do not start a new sentence with *but* or *so*. If you are connecting two short ideas with the other conjunctions, you may use a semicolon (;) rather than start a new sentence.
A nine-month school year has worked well; therefore, we should keep it.

 4 ► **Listen to the conversations. Does the second speaker in each conversation** *support the argument* **or** *counter the argument* **of the first speaker? Check (√) the correct column.**

SUPPORTS THE ARGUMENT   COUNTERS THE ARGUMENT

1. _____   _____
2. _____   _____
3. _____   _____
4. _____   _____
5. _____   _____

5 ► **The principal of a high school is going to give a speech to the students. Rewrite the speech, using at least three of these conjunctions:** *furthermore, moreover, however, nevertheless,* **and** *therefore.*

It has recently come to my attention that some students have not been attending classes regularly. This is a very serious situation. You cannot get good grades if you do not attend classes. You cannot qualify for a good job. It's true that many employers don't look at grades. Employers do want employees who are well educated, responsible, and have a positive attitude. I've heard several students say that classes are boring. If you have a positive attitude toward the material, you will see that it can be interesting. A good education is the most valuable of all possessions. I urge all of you to attend classes regularly.

6 ▶ **Study the frames: *Hope* vs. *wish* in past time**

Past time	Past tense form	
I might have passed the test. Tom might have quit his job.	**I hope**	I passed the test. Tom didn't quit his job.

Use *hope* to talk about something that possibly happened.

    I *hope I passed* the test. (I possibly did.)

Past time	Past perfect form	
I didn't pass the test. Tom quit his job. I couldn't take a vacation.	**I wish**	I had (I'd) passed the test. Tom hadn't quit his job. I could have taken a vacation.

Use *wish* to talk about something that's contrary-to-fact.

    I *wish I'd passed* the test. (I didn't.)

7 ▶ **Listen to the conversation.**
    ▶ **Act out similar conversations with a partner. Use the information in the box or your own information.**

A I wish I'd learned to play a musical instrument when I was young. I love classical music, and I've always wanted to play in an orchestra.

B Well, it's not too late. I know you have a busy schedule, but maybe you should consider taking music lessons. What instrument would you learn to play?

> Do you wish you . . .
>
> had learned to play a musical instrument?
> had majored in a different subject?
> had known your grandparents (better)?
> had stayed in touch with your old friends?
> hadn't moved when you were young?
> hadn't taken your current job?

8 ▶ **Read about these people, and say what they hope and wish about the past.**
    ▶ **Compare your answers with a partner.**

1. Eileen O'Brien wasn't paying attention while she was driving, and she hit a big pothole. She is afraid she might have damaged her car.
   Eileen wishes ⎯⎯⎯⎯⎯ .
   She hopes ⎯⎯⎯⎯⎯ .

2. Marie Laporte finally wrote to her friend Stella after three years. Two months later, she still hadn't gotten an answer, and now she's afraid Stella may have moved.
   Marie hopes ⎯⎯⎯⎯⎯ .
   She wishes ⎯⎯⎯⎯⎯ .

3. George Burke gave a speech yesterday. When he got home, he realized he'd left his briefcase in the auditorium.
   George hopes ⎯⎯⎯⎯⎯ .
   He wishes ⎯⎯⎯⎯⎯ .

4. Masa Asato wanted to keep working full time, but his company asked him to retire. Masa had an interview to be a part-time consultant at another company.
   Masa wishes ⎯⎯⎯⎯⎯ .
   He hopes ⎯⎯⎯⎯⎯ .

4. Your turn

Read the newspaper articles. The highlighted words are important for understanding the articles. Try to guess the meaning of the words from the context of the articles. As you read, form your own opinion on these issues: censorship of violence in video games, physical punishment of children in school, and government funding for the arts. Then, working in groups, argue for or against one or more of the issues. Try to support your argument with information in the articles or with your own examples.

VIOLENCE IN VIDEO GAMES

White Pine, Wyoming, usually a quiet town, was the scene of controversy last weekend as a parent group tried to ban the sale of violent video games.

Twenty parents, carrying signs saying "Stop the Violence Before It Begins" and "Protect Our Children Now," demonstrated in front of several stores where video games are sold.

The parent group said that video games have become increasingly violent because of advances in computer technology. "The violence in video games is worse than the violence on TV," one member of the group said. "When children are playing these games, they are actively participating in violent acts." For example, in one popular game whose goal is to become the world's best fighter, the characters' heads are torn off and their hearts are ripped out.

Teenagers who were interviewed outside one store were outraged by the demonstration. "To assume that young people will do whatever they see doesn't say much for their intelligence," said Greg Bryant, 16. "I should be able to buy any game that I choose," said Shelly Woods, 18. "If the demonstrators are against violent video games, they shouldn't buy them for their children. Censorship is not the answer."

Listen in

Read the statements below. Then listen to a radio discussion. Based on the opinions you hear, decide which person would be more likely to make each statement. Say *Ms. Young* or *Dr. Torres*.

1. Children who move all the time may have trouble in school.
2. People who move a lot are more tolerant and open-minded.
3. Children who move a lot find it easier to get used to new situations later in life.
4. Moving frequently can put a lot of stress on a couple's marriage.

Family Sues School for Slapping Child

A Westway couple was awarded $15,000 by a circuit judge after their ten year old accidentally had a tooth knocked out when he was slapped by his teacher, Mrs. Gertrude Wells, 47.

In his testimony, Robert Farrington, 10, described how his teacher had slapped him across the face for bringing a live frog into the classroom and "creating a serious disruption."

Mrs. Wells may face suspension, depending on the decision of the local school board.

"I am extremely sorry about the tooth," commented Mrs. Wells, "and I did not mean to lose control. This child, however, was always misbehaving. I was really fed up with him. This was the third time in a week I had lost at least a half hour of class time because of his behavior."

LOW INCOME HOUSING FOR ARTISTS APPROVED

SAN FRANCISCO, CA., May 30—The housing commission has approved the conversion of two apartment buildings on Sunrise Street to low-income housing for artists, writers, and people in the performing arts.

Although some local artists felt the decision was "long overdue," there was a great deal of opposition in the community. "These buildings provided low-income housing for poor families," said one area resident. "They will be forced out into the street."

"I feel sorry for the families who will have to move," commented Sally Fisher, a dancer. "However, if the arts are going to survive, the government will have to support them."

5. On your own

1. **Listen to people's opinions about the different issues in the box below. Then form your own opinions and agree or disagree with the ones stated.**

- a ban on smoking in public places
- a twelve-month school year
- criminals doing service in the community
- universal health coverage

2. **Write an editorial for a newspaper, choosing one of the options below.**

1. Give your opinion on one of the issues you discussed in Lesson 4. Support your arguments, counter any opposing arguments, and then draw a conclusion.

2. Support your point of view on any issue that is of concern to you. Draw a conclusion if possible.

PREVIEW

FUNCTIONS/THEMES	LANGUAGE	FORMS
Describe yourself Describe someone else	How would you describe yourself? I'm a reliable person. I consider myself hardworking. What do you think of him? I can't see him working with kids. He seems too indecisive.	Verbs followed by direct objects + noun, adjective, or verb complements
Make a recommendation	Why don't you go to Mario Zanelli? Mario always cuts my hair however I ask him to.	Question words with -ever

Preview the reading.

1. Work with a partner. Do you know the name of the man in the photo below? He is famous for fighting against discrimination. What does the word *discrimination* mean? In what areas of the world is there discrimination?

2. Before you read the article on pages 12–13, look at the title and the photos. How do you think the article will relate to discrimination? Discuss your ideas with a partner.

Jesse Owens

An Athlete's Life in Retrospect

by Frank Litsky

Jesse Owens receiving a gold medal at the 1936 Olympic Games.

Jesse Owens, whose four gold medals at the 1936 Olympic Games in Berlin made him perhaps the greatest and most famous athlete in track and field history, never received much recognition at the time of his success. The victim of racial discrimination and of the times in which he lived, Owens ultimately created his place in history through his own inner courage and determination. Today Owens is remembered not only as a great athlete, but as someone with great moral integrity who believed in the old-fashioned values of honesty and hard work.

■ Father Was a Sharecropper

James Cleveland Owens was born September 12, 1913, in Danville, Alabama, the son of a sharecropper and the grandson of slaves. The youngster picked cotton until he and his family moved to Cleveland when he was 9. There, a schoolteacher asked the youth his name.

"J.C." he replied.

She thought he had said "Jesse," and he had a new name.

He ran his first race at age 13. After high school, he went to Ohio State University, paying his way as a $100-a-month night elevator operator because he had no athletic scholarship. As a sophomore, in the Big Ten championship games in 1935, he set even more records than he would in his Olympic glory a year later.

A week before the Big Ten meet, Owens accidentally fell down a flight of stairs. His back hurt so much that he could not exercise all week, and he had to be helped in and out of the car that drove him to the Big Ten meet. In an unsuccessful attempt to lessen the back pain, Owens sat for a half hour in a hot tub. He still rejected suggestions that he withdraw and said he would try, event by event.

He did try, and the results are in the record book. On May 25, 1935, Jesse Owens equaled the world record for the 100-yard dash (9.4 seconds), broke the world record for the broad jump (now called the long jump) with his only attempt (26 feet 8 1/4 inches), broke the world record for the 220-yard dash (20.3 seconds), and broke the world record for the 220-yard low hurdles (22.6 seconds).

■ Overcomes Racial Prejudice

The stage was set for Owens's victory at the Olympic Games in Berlin the next year, and his triumph would come to be regarded as not only athletic but also political. Although Adolph Hitler had intended the Berlin games to reinforce the Nazi doctrine of Aryan supremacy, the United States Olympic track team of 66 athletes included ten African-Americans, and six of the individual gold medals in track won by American men were won by black athletes. Owens was the hero, winning the 100-meter dash in 10.3 seconds, the 200-meter dash in 20.7 seconds, and the broad jump at 26 feet 5 1/2 inches. He also headed the United States team that won the 400-meter relay in 39.8 seconds.

Hitler did not congratulate any of the African-American winners, a subject to which Mr. Owens addressed himself for the rest of his life.

"It was all right with me," he said years later. "I didn't go to Berlin to shake hands with him, anyway. All I know is that I'm here now and Hitler isn't."

Having returned from Berlin, he received no telephone call from the president of his own country, either. In fact, he was not honored by the United States until 1976, four years before his death, when he was awarded the Presidential Medal of Freedom. Three years later, he received the Living Legends Award.

There were no big contracts for Owens after his Olympic victories. He became a playground janitor because he could not find another job. He ended his career as an amateur runner and accepted money to race against cars, trucks, motorcycles, and dogs.

"Sure, it bothered me," he said later. "But at least it was an honest living. I had to eat."

In time, however, his gold medals changed his life. "They have kept me alive over the years," he once said. "Time has stood still for me. That golden moment dies hard."

■ **Celebrated as a Speaker**

By many, Owens will be best remembered as a public speaker. Despite his personal disappointments, his speeches praised the virtues of patriotism, clean living, and fair play. His delivery was spellbinding, and he was once described as a "full-time banquet guest, what you might call a professional good example."

Jesse Owens died of cancer in 1980, at the age of 66. Although Owens was ignored at the time of his success, his personal triumph over prejudice is perhaps best expressed in this statement, which was issued by [United States] President Carter at the time of his death:

"Perhaps no athlete better symbolized the human struggle against tyranny, poverty, and racial bigotry."

Jesse Owens receiving the Presidential Medal of Freedom from United States President Gerald Ford, 1976.

Jesse Owens in a parade in Cleveland, Ohio.

Figure it out

1. As you read the article, look for facts that support each of the statements below. When you have finished reading, give at least two facts that support each statement.

1. Jesse Owens was a man with a great deal of determination who did not give up easily.
2. Jesse Owens was discriminated against because he was black.
3. Over time people's feelings and attitudes toward Jesse Owens changed a great deal.

2. Based on your interpretation of the article, explain the meaning of the sentence below.

Jesse Owens's triumph [in the 1936 Olympic Games] would come to be regarded as not only athletic but also political.

3. Look at the following statements, quoted from the article, that Jesse Owens made. Then explain in a few sentences what you think these statements as a group say about Owens's attitude toward life.

1. "I didn't go to Berlin to shake hands with [Hitler], anyway. All I know is that I'm here now and Hitler isn't."
2. "Sure, it bothered me [that I couldn't find a better job.] But at least it was an honest living. I had to eat."
3. "[My gold medals] have kept me alive over the years. Time has stood still for me. That golden moment dies hard."

4. Both the suffixes -ic, as in *athletic*, and -al, as in *personal*, are used to form adjectives from nouns. Use five words from the list to write sentences about Jesse Owens.

athletic	patriotic	professional	racial
financial	personal	Olympic	political

7. You really surprise me.

1. What kind of person does each of these jobs require? Explain to your partner why you would or would not be the right person for one of them.

an athletic instructor   a department store salesperson   a diplomat
a night security guard   a tour guide   a flight attendant

Bill, a tennis instructor at a community center, is talking to his friend Vanessa.

Listen to the conversation.

②

Bill   Hey, have you heard? Robert is retiring.

Vanessa   Oh, really? Well, maybe you'll be made athletic director. Keep your fingers crossed.

Bill   Oh, I hope not. Whoever they choose is fine as long as it's not me. I'm the wrong person for that job!

Vanessa   Why do you say that? I mean, what kind of person does it take?

Bill   Someone with a more easygoing personality.

Vanessa   Oh, come on. You seem like someone who could handle anything.

Bill   Me? You've got to be kidding. That job would make me much too nervous. Besides, I'm happy with things the way they are. I consider teaching tennis a challenge. It's a chance to get people interested in sports.

Vanessa   You really surprise me. I always thought you were more ambitious.

Bill   Not really. I take pride in my work. Whatever I do, I like to do well, but I wouldn't call that ambition.

Vanessa   So, you really don't think you're cut out for it?

Bill   No, I really don't. I just can't imagine myself managing a staff and worrying about finances. I don't handle pressure too well.

Vanessa   You know, that's not the impression I have of you at all. That's how I'd describe myself!

3. Say *True, False,* or *It doesn't say.*

1. Bill thinks the athletic director should be easygoing and able to handle pressure.
2. Vanessa thinks Bill is cut out for the job of athletic director.
3. Vanessa would like the job herself.
4. Bill considers himself ambitious.
5. Vanessa thinks she handles pressure well.

8. I consider myself hardworking.

1 ▶ Listen to part of a job interview.
▶ Act out a similar interview with a partner. Describe yourself using the descriptions and characteristics in the boxes or your own information. Remember, at an interview you should mention only your *positive* characteristics.

A How would you describe yourself?
B I'm a reliable person. I consider myself hardworking and creative. I enjoy responsibility and I handle pressure well.

Some descriptions
Positive
I'm a reliable person.
I consider myself hardworking.
I enjoy responsibility/a challenge.
I handle pressure well.
Negative
I can't see/imagine him working with kids.
Kids make her nervous.
His coworkers consider him unreliable.
She seems like someone who wouldn't be a good teacher.

Some personal characteristics	
Positive	**Negative**
ambitious	unambitious
cooperative	uncooperative
creative	unimaginative
hardworking	lazy
independent	indecisive
modest	conceited
outgoing, friendly	unfriendly
patient	impatient
reliable, responsible	unreliable, irresponsible
self-confident	insecure
honest, sincere	insincere

2 ▶ You have interviewed three people for one of the jobs in the box below. Using the information in your notes, discuss the job candidates with your partner. You may also use the descriptions and characteristics in exercise 1.

A I interviewed Bob Morgan yesterday to be our new physical education teacher.
B Oh, I've seen his résumé. What did you think of him?
A He really didn't impress me. To tell you the truth, I can't see him working with kids. He seems too indecisive.
B Have you heard anything about him?
A Nothing very positive. His coworkers consider him unreliable, and I've heard he doesn't handle responsibility too well.

1. **Bob Morgan**
   • indecisive
   • coworkers say he's unreliable
   • not good with responsibility
   • hates pressure

2. **Marta Velez**
   • self-confident
   • colleagues say she's hardworking
   • enjoys a challenge
   • seems very honest and sincere

3. **Lucy Como**
   • conceited, but creative
   • friends say she's impatient
   • hates tight deadlines
   • previous boss says she's uncooperative

Some jobs
a physical education teacher
an art director for the new magazine, *The Great Outdoors*
a sales manager for a computer company
a social director for a large resort hotel
a flight attendant for a major international airline
a nontechnical worker to assist a research team in the Sahara Desert

DESCRIBE YOURSELF • DESCRIBE SOMEONE ELSE • VERBS FOLLOWED BY DIRECT OBJECTS + NOUN, ADJECTIVE, OR VERB COMPLEMENTS

3

- ▶ **Rate yourself on the chart below. Write *1*, *2*, or *3*.**
- ▶ **Discuss with a partner why you would or would not be the right person for one of the jobs in exercise 2, using the personal characteristics from the chart.**

I think I'd be a good art director because I consider myself creative and outgoing.

1 = very 2 = average 3 = not at all

ambitious	_____	modest	_____
cooperative	_____	outgoing, friendly	_____
creative	_____	patient	_____
hardworking	_____	reliable, responsible	_____
honest, sincere	_____	self-confident	_____
independent	_____		

4

▶ **Study the frames: Verbs followed by direct objects + noun, adjective, or verb complements**

They	appointed	**him**	**director**.
They	made	**her**	**supervisor**.

▲ noun

They	consider	**me**	**reliable**.
My job	keeps	**me**	**busy**.

▲ adjective

I	can't see	**him**	**working**	with kids.
They	make	**him**	**lose**	his patience.

▲ verb

Some verbs and their possible complements

Verb	Noun	Adjective	Base form of verb	Progressive form of verb
appoint	√			
call	√	√		
consider	√	√		
elect	√			
find		√		√
hear			√	√
imagine				√
keep		√		√
make	√	√	√	
see			√	√
watch			√	√

Sense verbs, such as *hear* and *see*, may be followed by either base or progressive forms of verbs.

5

▶ **Rewrite the obituary, completing each sentence with one item from column A and one from column B. Make sure to use the correct tense of the verbs in column A.**

Column A	Column B
elect her	doing
watch her	my closest friend
can't imagine myself	laughing and playing
consider her	genuinely sincere
keep me	happy
found her	a lifetime member
make everyone	busy

SONIA MERENDA

Sonia Merenda, who founded the Society for Orphaned Children 62 years ago, died last week after a long illness. For over 60 years, Mrs. Merenda was a dedicated worker at the Society, and last year, the Society *elected her a lifetime member* for her long years of service.

At a memorial service for Mrs. Merenda on Sunday, people expressed their fond memories. "Mrs. Merenda was so good to me as a child," said Claude Duval, now 34. "For many years I _____ . I never lost touch with her, and I would visit her often." Mr. Duval's wife, Miriam, remembers the first time she met Mrs. Merenda. "I _____ , the kind of person everyone likes," she said. "I once _____ with the children for over an hour. She seemed to _____ ."

Sonia Merenda continued to work until several months ago. "My work _____ seven days a week," she said in an interview last year. "But I _____ anything else."

Sonia Merenda will be missed by all of us. Expressions of sympathy may be mailed to the Society for Orphaned Children.

6 ▶ **Listen to the conversation between two sales managers. Check (√) the characteristics they want in a job candidate.**

7 ▶ **Study the frames: Question words with *-ever***

Whoever we hire should be reliable. He gets along with **who(m)ever** he meets.	I get nervous **whenever** I give a speech. **Whenever** I talk to my boss, I get nervous.	Question words with *-ever* give the idea of "any." *whoever* we hire = *anyone* we hire
She enjoys **whatever** she does. **Whatever** I do, I do well.	He's done well **wherever** he's worked. **Wherever** I go, I have a good time.	where + ever = wherever
We can go to **whichever** movie you prefer. **Whichever** one you want to see is fine.	I go to work **however** I feel, sick or not. **However** I feel, I go to work.	

8 ▶ **Complete the conversation, using question words with *-ever*.**
  ▶ **Listen to check your work.**
  ▶ **Practice the conversation with a partner.**

A My hairdresser is just awful. _____ I ask him to do, he always seems to do something else. I've never had a good hairdresser, in fact. I just seem to have bad luck _____ I go.
B Listen, I know of two very good hairdressers. . . .
A Well, I'd prefer to try _____ one is less expensive.
B Then why don't you go to Mario Zanelli? The name of the place is Zanelli Hair Stylists, and it's at 43 Deco Street.

A That's right near where I work.
B I'm sure you'll be satisfied. Mario always cuts my hair _____ I ask him to. And he's almost always available _____ I want to make an appointment.
A Great! Thanks a lot for the recommendation.

9 ▶ **Often, when you apply to go to a college, to get a scholarship, or for a job, you are asked to write a short essay about yourself. Read the model essay. Then follow the instructions on the application form and write about yourself.**

THE BRUBANK CORPORATION

Name CYNTHIA J. COGGINS

In 200 words or less, describe yourself. What are your strengths? What are your weaknesses?

I am a very reliable and conscientious person. Whenever I have a job to do, I try to do it to the best of my ability. I like responsibility and I enjoy challenges. I try to find creative solutions to problems.

All of my life, I have gotten a great deal of personal satisfaction from my work. I enjoy working with others as well as alone. I am sincere and I am fair. My classmates and colleagues consider me kind and understanding.

Unfortunately, though, I have a major shortcoming. I am not always patient. People who do not do their full share of the work make me angry. I think people in school or at work have a responsibility to others, and I can't see myself working with people who are unreliable.

I realize this description may make me sound somewhat conceited and demanding. Actually, I am a very modest person, but in order to give you an accurate picture of myself, I have tried to be very honest. In any case, I feel that whatever I do and wherever I go, I have the personal characteristics that will make me successful.

9. Your turn

You and a group of classmates work for the Foreign Student Placement Service (FSPS). You have three applications from foreign students who want to live and study for a year in the United States. Unfortunately, you only have one application from a family that would like to host a foreign student. Look at the student information cards below, and read the letter from the family on page 19. Then, working in groups, discuss the different students and decide which one to place with the family.

FOREIGN STUDENT PLACEMENT SERVICE

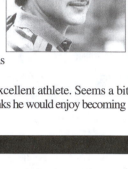

1. **NAME** Paulo Serrador
2. **ADDRESS** Rua da Bahia, 1723/Belo Horizonte, Brazil
3. **AGE** 15
4. **HEALTH** Excellent
5. **FAMILY BACKGROUND** Father, owner of small grocery store; mother, nurse; no brothers or sisters
6. **SCHOOL INFORMATION** Serious student who tries hard, but receives only average grades in all subjects
7. **ENGLISH PROFICIENCY** Speaks excellent English (has many American, British, and Australian friends)
8. **INTERESTS AND HOBBIES** Swimming, soccer, camping; has played in several national soccer competitions
9. **REFERENCES** Four excellent references from teachers (see file)
10. **COMMENTS** Very outgoing and confident, well liked by his teachers and fellow students. Also an excellent athlete. Seems a bit indecisive about his future, but plans to go to college after high school. He isn't sure what he'll study, but he thinks he would enjoy becoming an English teacher.

FOREIGN STUDENT PLACEMENT SERVICE

1. **NAME** Lucia Morales
2. **ADDRESS** Apartado Posal 995/Guatemala, Guatemala, C.A.
3. **AGE** 16
4. **HEALTH** Excellent
5. **FAMILY BACKGROUND** Father, doctor; mother, housewife; sister, 14, in high school; sister, 20, studying accounting in college; brother, 18, works for national airline
6. **SCHOOL INFORMATION** Excellent student, top of her class in chemistry and biology; very good grades in other subjects
7. **ENGLISH PROFICIENCY** Cannot speak English well, but has a good knowledge of grammar; currently enrolled in a private English conversation class after school
8. **INTERESTS AND HOBBIES** Reading and classical music
9. **REFERENCES** Three impressive letters from current teachers and two from the hospital where she has worked as a nurse's aide during school vacations (see file)
10. **COMMENTS** Hardworking student who wants to be a doctor like her father. Very conscientious in her schoolwork and part-time jobs, but shy. Wants to learn English and feels it would be easier to do so living with an English-speaking family.

FOREIGN STUDENT PLACEMENT SERVICE

1. **NAME** Michio Yoshimura
2. **ADDRESS** 66 Banchi/ Aza Kawaguchi/Oaza-Yamashita/ Himeji City, Japan
3. **AGE** 16
4. **HEALTH** Excellent, but walks with crutches (right leg crippled at birth)
5. **FAMILY BACKGROUND** Father, farmer; mother, housewife; sister, 11, in primary school; brother, 22, high-school history teacher and swimming coach
6. **SCHOOL INFORMATION** Very serious student, excellent grades in science and math; average grades in other subjects
7. **ENGLISH PROFICIENCY** Speaks English with difficulty, but would learn quickly if he had more contact with English speakers
8. **INTERESTS AND HOBBIES** Repairs his friends' radios and stereos; president of science club; excellent swimmer
9. **REFERENCES** Excellent references from four teachers (see file)
10. **COMMENTS** Serious student who is ambitious and determined. Would like to become an electrical engineer and wants to learn English well enough to go to college in the United States after he finishes high school. Very energetic and outgoing in spite of handicap.

Mr. Steven Compton
Foreign Student Placement Service
870 North Michigan Avenue
Chicago, Illinois 60626

150 Cedar Drive
Naperville, Illinois 60565

Dear Mr. Compton:

I am returning our application to host a foreign student for the coming school year. My husband, John, and I are looking forward to this special visit, and our son and daughter are as excited as we are about sharing our home. We think we have a great deal to offer, both intellectually and socially, to a foreign student.

As you can see from the enclosed application, our family is ambitious and hardworking, but we are also very sports-minded. As we mentioned under "Interests and Hobbies," John coaches the Sacramento Flyers (the high school soccer team) and my daughter, Debbie, is on the high school swimming team. One thing that I forgot to mention on the application is that the entire family goes camping several times a year. We all enjoy the outdoors a great deal.

The application didn't ask for the length of time we have been at our jobs, but I would like to mention that my husband has been teaching English for twelve years, and I have been a nurse at Mercy Hospital for almost four years. Our son, John Jr., works part time also. He has had an afternoon paper route for the past two years. Also, there was no place on the application for me to mention that Debbie won the Freshman Class Science Prize this year. She was extremely pleased and has decided to major in computer electronics when she goes to college.

I think the application covers everything else. However, I did want you to know as much about us as possible. We are all looking forward to hearing from you.

Sincerely,

Beth Ann Kozinski

Beth Ann Kozinski

🔊 Listen in

Read the statements below. Then listen to the conversation between Steven Compton and Ana Cruz, employees at the Foreign Student Placement Service, as they finish lunch. Choose *a* or *b*.

1. Ana takes her job
   a. seriously.
   b. casually.

2. Ana's horoscope says
   a. success will come to her soon.
   b. she'll soon fall in love.

3. Steven's horoscope says he's
   a. conscientious and reliable.
   b. very romantic.

4. Steven thinks of himself as someone
   a. very reliable.
   b. lazy and irresponsible.

10. On your own

1. Write a two- or three- paragraph letter to the Kozinskis, the family who would like to host a foreign student. In the letter, describe the FSPS applicant that you have chosen to stay with them. Tell why you have selected this applicant.

2. **Choose one of the following tasks.**

1. You have been placed with the Kozinski family. You plan to live with them while you study in the United States. Write them a letter describing yourself.

2. You have been assigned a pen pal in an English-speaking country. Write a letter to him or her describing yourself.

PREVIEW

FUNCTIONS/THEMES	LANGUAGE	FORMS
Convince someone Inform someone	I don't really need a footrest. Even so, I suggest that you try it out. You won't find a better buy. It's important that the boss not realize you're behind. It's necessary that we finish the work today.	Some verbs and expressions that require the subjunctive
Make a purchase	I'd like to think it over. I'd like to think about it.	Two-word verbs

Preview the reading.

1. **Student A**   You are selling the used items shown in the picture. Student B will ask you some questions about one of the items. Answer the questions and try to give Student B several good reasons to buy the item.
   Student B   You are interested in buying one of the used items in the picture. Ask Student A some questions about it. Decide whether or not you want to buy it.

2. Before you read the article on pages 22–23, look at the title and photos and explain what you think the purpose of a flea market is. Then read the first two paragraphs. Does your answer change?

11. Flea Market

by Cree McCree

A typical weekend crowd at a flea market.

① On any weekend at sunrise, while most of the country still sleeps, vans, pickup trucks, campers, and cars crammed with every conceivable item gather in empty parking lots, fairgrounds, and drive-in movie theaters across the U.S. By noon, the scene overflows with thousands of people who have come to bargain and browse at this mad carnival called a flea market.

② People have traded and bartered for centuries. Whatever else the flea market may appear to be, its purpose is the sale and exchange of goods. Whether they are knowledgeable collectors or just plain bargain hunters, people are drawn to the flea market by the enormous amount and variety of merchandise offered. The possibility of finding something truly valuable before anybody else does makes shopping at a flea market a treasure hunt.

③ For many buyers, the ritual of bargaining at a flea market is as much fun as the bargain itself. It's not just the money they save that gives them a warm inner glow of accomplishment; it's the satisfaction of playing an ancient game.

④ Satisfaction also comes from the immediacy of a flea-market exchange. After you negotiate your price, it is "cash and carry"—the dealer pockets your money, you go home with your purchase, and that's that. You got what you wanted, and the dealer got what he or she wanted. In today's world of credit cards, the flea market takes you back to a time when life was simpler and money had more meaning.

⑤ There's magic in a place where anything can happen. The flea market allows us to be children again, to play dress-up and try on funny hats, and to embark on an adventure of discovery and surprise. It also allows us to reclaim items from our past that have been swept away by time, only to reappear again, almost miraculously, at the market.

⑥ The variety of people who set up stalls at the flea market often rivals the variety of the merchandise. These vendors may have nothing in common during their weekday lives, but over the weekend their diversity becomes community. A couple sells embroidered slippers next to a teenager displaying cat's-eye sunglasses across from another dealer's car hubcaps, baby dolls, and plastic potted plants. On the street, they would probably never talk to each other. Here they do.

⑦ What do these "fleas" have in common here? Perhaps

A woman shopping at a flea market.

A vendor displaying her merchandise.

it is a belief in getting ahead, in becoming economically self-sufficient, and in taking control of their own lives. Vendors willingly give up the security of a nine-to-five job in exchange for freedom: freedom from rigid working hours; freedom from the world of inflation; freedom to choose when, where, and what they will sell; freedom to be what they want to be.

⑧ Yet the flea market is much more than an odd mixture of people selling a hodgepodge of products. "This is a serious enterprise," says vendor Joel Kaufmann of New York. "The amount of labor and organization that goes into an operation like this is phenomenal." Perhaps most important to the flea market's success is the spirit of cooperation among vendors. "At the flea market, everyone is encouraged to be an individual, [but, at the same time,] to help each other out," says Caggie Daniels of Santa Fe, New Mexico. "It's a shame cities aren't run like this."

Figure it out

1. As you read, look for the answers to these questions. When you have finished, try to answer the questions without looking back at the article. Do exercise 2 before correcting your answers.

1. How is shopping at a flea market different from shopping at a regular store?
2. What are some of the reasons that people enjoy shopping at a flea market?
3. How are the vendors at a flea market different from each other? How are they alike?
4. What makes flea markets operate successfully?

2. Find at least one paragraph that makes each of the following main points. Then use your answers to this exercise to help you check and correct your answers to exercise 1.

1. The variety of merchandise at a flea market offers its shoppers many surprises.
2. Flea markets work so well because everyone cooperates with each other.
3. Many people enjoy the game of bargaining just as much as the money they end up saving.
4. The flea market is, in fact, a business whose main purpose is to sell merchandise.
5. Although vendors may seem to have nothing in common, they share similar beliefs and values.
6. Many people enjoy the flea market because, in various ways, it reminds them of the past.

3. The suffixes -ity and, in some cases, -ty, are used to form nouns from many adjectives. Use five words from the list to write sentences about flea markets.

activity	certainty	community
diversity	possibility	security

12. You're welcome to think it over.

1. **Your partner has just inherited $25,000 from his or her grandfather. Your partner, who is unemployed, wants to buy a car. Try to convince him or her that it would be best to put the money in the bank.**

 A salesperson in a furniture store is trying to sell Rita Rollins a sofa bed.

Listen to the conversation.

2

Rita Excuse me. I'm looking for a comfortable sofa bed for a guest room . . . .

Salesperson Yes, ma'am! I've got just the sofa bed you're looking for. Isn't this a beauty? It's on sale today for $499.

Rita Hmm . . . It's pretty comfortable to sit on. How comfortable is the bed?

Salesperson Here, let me open it for you to try out . . . .

Rita Yes, the bed's not too bad . . . . I'd like to think it over, though. It's not exactly what I had in mind.

Salesperson I can assure you that you won't find anything more reasonable or more comfortable. And this is the ideal sofa bed for a guest room. It's important that your guests be comfortable, right?

Rita Yes, but I'm worried about the color. White gets dirty so easily, and you know how guests are sometimes . . . .

Salesperson Oh, this fabric doesn't stain very easily. A little soap and water will remove any spots. Of course, it's essential that you get them out right away . . . the stains that is, not the guests! *(Laughs)*

Rita Well . . .

Salesperson Look, a few weeks ago another customer had his doubts when I suggested that he buy one of these sofa beds. But do you think he brought it back? No way! In fact, he called me up and ordered another one.

Rita Well . . . it *is* comfortable . . . Uh . . . but I think I'll look around and then decide.

Salesperson You're welcome to think it over, but I can't guarantee that it'll still be here if you decide to come back.

Rita Oh, is this the only one you have?

Salesperson It's the last one we have in stock. They've been selling like crazy.

Rita Still, I'll have to think about it. It's a big purchase.

Salesperson O.K. I just hope you make the right decision.

3. **Check (√) the statements that are stated or implied in the conversation.**

____ Rita wants to buy a sofa bed.
____ Rita needs a sofa bed for her living room.
____ The sofa bed in the store comes in white or black.
____ Rita isn't sure she wants to buy the sofa bed.

____ The salesperson says the sofa bed is easy to clean.
____ The salesperson tries to convince Rita by talking about a satisfied customer.
____ Rita buys the sofa bed before leaving the store.

13. I suggest that you try it out.

1 ▶ **Listen to the conversation.**
  ▶ **Act out similar conversations. You are looking to buy one of the items in the illustrations below. Your partner is a salesperson and will try to sell you the item.**

A Hello, I'm looking for an easy chair, preferably in a dark color.
B Well, this one is on sale. It even comes with a footrest.
A Hmm . . . I don't really need a footrest. I have a small apartment.
B Even so, I suggest that you try it out. You won't find a better buy. If you don't like it, you don't have to buy it.
A Well, O.K. Let me try it out.

Some objections
I don't really need a _____ .
It doesn't match my furniture.
It's the wrong shape/size for my apartment.
The color/style isn't exactly what I had in mind.

Some suggestions
Try it out.
Look it over.
See if you like it.
See how it works.

easy chair with footrest

computer desk with chair

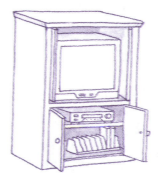

TV/VCR cabinet with video rack

bookcase with pull-out desk

2 ▶ **Listen to the conversation.**
  ▶ **Act out similar conversations, using the information and expressions in the boxes. Your partner is a friend who you are concerned about. Try to find out what's wrong and convince your friend to do something about it.**

A Is everything O.K., Shelly? I've noticed you haven't been concentrating on your work.
B This job is just so boring . . . .
A I know, but you know that we have to get things done on time here. It's important that the boss not realize you're behind.
B Yeah, I suppose you're right.
A Personally, I think you should work a little later tonight to catch up. It's up to you, though.
B But we were supposed to go to the movies tonight, remember?
A Feel free to cancel if you want. It's more important that you get your work done.

Some situations at work
Your partner hasn't been concentrating and is behind in his or her work.
Your partner dislikes another employee, but the two of them have to work together.
Your partner finds the work too difficult, but is too embarrassed to ask for help.
Your partner shares an office with someone who receives frequent personal phone calls.

Some ways to convince someone
It's important that . . .
It's essential that . . .
I (strongly) suggest that . . .
I propose that . . .

▲

These expressions are followed by a subject pronoun and the base form of the verb.

3 ▶ Listen to the conversations. Check (√) the drawings that correspond to conversations in which one speaker is trying to convince the other.

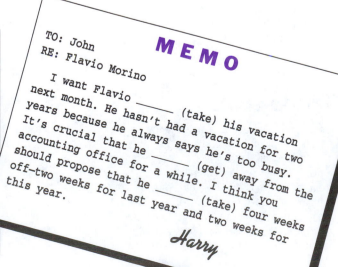

4 ▶ Study the frame: Some verbs and expressions that require the subjunctive

They	recommend suggest insist propose	that	I you he she we they	be plan finish set	on time. a meeting. the work today. a schedule.
It's	important necessary essential crucial				

▲ subject pronoun   ▲ base form

Compare:
They insisted *that we be* on time.
They wanted *us to be* on time.

5 ▶ Rewrite these memos from the manager of a department store to two of his employees, completing them with the correct forms of the verbs in parentheses.

M E M O

Alice,

It is essential that I _____ (hire) another salesperson to help you in the electronics department. The employment agency recommended that I _____ (interview) a Mr. Murray. He will come in tomorrow at 2:00. Although I realize that you _____ (be) very busy, it is important that he _____ (meet) you, so I'll bring him to your department at about 2:30.

Harry

M E M O

TO: John
RE: Flavio Morino

I want Flavio _____ (take) his vacation next month. He hasn't had a vacation for two years because he always says he's too busy. It's crucial that he _____ (get) away from the accounting office for a while. I think you should propose that he _____ (take) four weeks off—two weeks for last year and two weeks for this year.

Harry

6 ▶ **Study the frames: Two-word verbs**

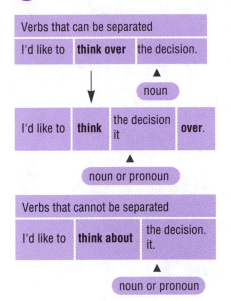

Verbs that can be separated		
I'd like to	**think over**	the decision.

↓ → noun

I'd like to	**think**	the decision it	**over**.

↑ noun or pronoun

Verbs that cannot be separated		
I'd like to	**think about**	the decision. it.

↑ noun or pronoun

Some separable verbs		
bring back	look up	think over
call up	pick out	try out
figure out	pick up	turn off
fill in	put on	turn on
fill out	take back	write down
get back		

Some inseparable verbs		
ask for	look for	talk about
go over	plan for	think about
hear from	run into	worry about

7 ▶ **Complete the conversation between the salesperson and the customer, using the items in the box. Pay attention to whether the verb can be separated, and make sure you place the pronouns correctly.**

think about/the cassette player	bring back/it	run into/any major difficulty
think over/it	ask for/me	look up/it

Salesperson Enjoy your stereo.
Customer Thanks. Oh, by the way, what should I do if I have any trouble with it?
Salesperson Well, if you have any trouble during the first three months, I suggest that you just _____ . After that, if you _____ with it, Mitsuyo will guarantee free service and parts for a full year.

Customer O.K. By the way, where's the nearest Mitsuyo service center?
Salesperson Actually, I don't know. But you can _____ in the phone book.
Customer Thanks. And I'll _____ . I'm just not sure if I can afford it right now.
Salesperson All right. _____ and just _____ if you come back. I'll be happy to help you.

8 ▶ **Read the description below about a friend of yours who is planning to get married. Then write a short letter convincing your friend that he or she is making a big mistake.**

A good friend of yours who is very hardworking and very wealthy has decided to get married. The person he or she is marrying is unemployed and never has any money, but likes to dress well, go out to eat all the time, and go dancing at night. During the day, the person sleeps late and spends the rest of the time at the beach or playing tennis.

Although your friend likes to dance and play tennis, he or she is basically very domestic and likes to cook, eat at home, and go to bed early. He or she also likes to work, and often works long hours, sometimes even on the weekends.

14. Your turn

You and a group of classmates would like to take a vacation together. Read the descriptions of the two tours in the ads and look at the photos. Discuss the pros and cons of each trip, and then try to convince the other students in your group to take the trip that appeals to you more.

Listen in

A man is trying to convince a friend to take a vacation in Curaçao. Read the sentences below. Then listen to the conversation and choose *a* or *b*.

1. The man thinks Curaçao is
   a. too far.
   b. not far at all by plane.

2. The man thinks Curaçao is just
   a. a typical tropical island with a beach.
   b. like being in paradise.

3. The woman is
   a. excited about going to Curaçao.
   b. hesitant about going to Curaçao.

4. The man thinks Curaçao is
   a. relaxing because you can do whatever you want to do.
   b. exhausting because there is so much to do.

What kind of vacation do you enjoy? Do you prefer to go to a tropical resort? to the quiet countryside? to visit your relatives? Discuss these questions in groups.

CURAÇAO
GRAND GETAWAY
BARGAIN CHARTER TOURS

ONE WEEK ONLY $749*

This fabulous vacation includes:

- round-trip airfare from Miami, Florida
- bus from airport to hotel
- 7 nights at the Deluxe Beachfront Hotel
- special shopping discounts
- day tour of island
- dinner with a local family
- hotel entertainment

And much, much more!

Departures every Monday until June. Reserve now. Space is limited and tours sell out quickly!

*Vacation price based on double occupancy + 15% of indicated list price as tax and service charge.

Wilemstad, Curaçao

Wilemstad, Curaçao

Caracas, Venezuela

Curaçao + Fabulous Cruise
Caracas, San Juan, + Bermuda Option

You've never experienced anything like it!
Includes:

- round-trip flight from Miami to Curaçao
- cruise to exciting Caracas, San Juan,* and back to Curaçao
- all meals and entertainment
- swimming pool and health club
- supervised wind surfing and scuba diving available at only a small cost

All this without ever leaving the boat!
7 days/6 nights—Only $1,399**
Every day a new adventure!

*For the truly adventurous, fly from San Juan on to lovely Bermuda for an additional 3 days and 2 nights at the low, low cost of only $499.**
**Tax excluded; Bermuda extension includes return flight from Bermuda to Miami.

San Juan, Puerto Rico

Southhampton, Bermuda

15. On your own

1. Imagine that someone you know is reluctant to take a trip to your city or country. Write the person a letter describing your city or country, and try to convince him or her to come for a visit. Include any necessary information on making reservations. Also mention if it is necessary to make any special arrangements or preparations, such as getting a passport or visa.

2. Choose one of the items in the pictures. Write an advertisement that will convince people to buy that item.

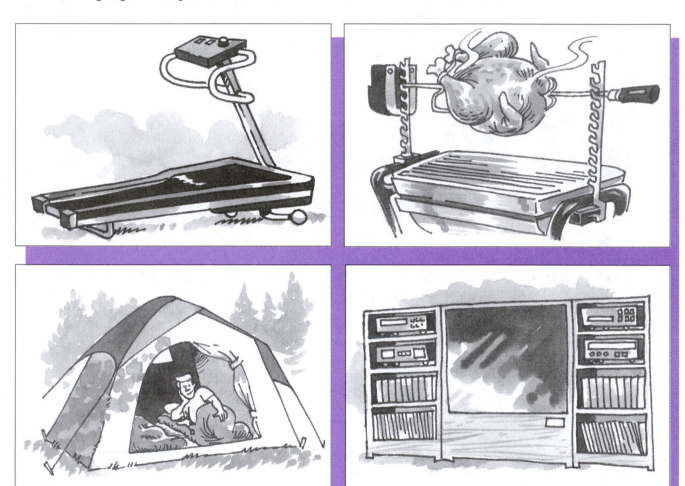

FUNCTIONS/THEMES	LANGUAGE	FORMS
Give instructions	First, you have to make the preflight inspection. Then, you start the engine. Once you've started the engine, you continue your checking.	Using time markers to put events in order
Explain something	After you start the engine, you contact ground control. When flying an airplane, you should be careful.	General statements with *before, after,* and *when*
Talk about interests	Before taking pottery classes, I used to make things out of leather. After I took flying lessons, I bought a plane.	Specific statements with *before, after, when,* and *while*

Preview the reading.

1. Work with a partner. What makes each of the trips in the pictures dangerous? Have you ever taken a trip that turned out to be dangerous? Tell your partner about it.

2. Before you read the article on page 32, look at the title and the illustration on pages 32–33. What do you think the word *perils* means? Discuss your ideas with a partner.

Balloonist Recalls Perils on First Pacific Crossing

by Wallace Turner

In its 6,000-mile Pacific crossing, the balloon *Double Eagle 5* hovered near disaster and narrowly avoided crashing into a street of homes in California, just minutes before a desperate landing on a mountain ridge. Ben Abruzzo was making the first attempt to cross the Pacific in a balloon with passengers. Also on the balloon were Larry Newman, 34, and Ron Clark, 41, both of Albuquerque, New Mexico; and Rocky Aoki, 42, owner of a restaurant chain, who financed the voyage.

When asked what the worst part of the trip was, Ben Abruzzo said, "All of it. We had a tough takeoff. . . . We picked up ice and couldn't get rid of it."

The rough voyage began in Nagashima, Japan, on November 10, and, according to Abruzzo, nothing worked as expected. "We picked up ice right away, and the weight [of the ice clinging to the balloon] kept us from getting our altitude," Abruzzo said. "We carried ice all across the Pacific." The crew repeatedly had to lighten the balloon by throwing out ballast—bags of sand that regulate the balloon's ascent and can be poured out to make the balloon lighter. Yet, not only was ballast being used up at a fast rate, but the balloon still couldn't climb because it had picked up more snow and ice. "Halfway across we were down to 4,500 feet when we should have been at 22,500 feet," Abruzzo said.

He said that if it hadn't been for the ice, "we would have made it to Europe easily." The balloonists had intended to land in a valley a few miles inland from the ocean, near Ukiah, California. Because of the ice, however, the balloon could not cross the mountains to the east.

"So we started coming down," Abruzzo said, "and when we broke through [the clouds] we could see this street of homes, with the lights on, and I knew we couldn't come down there." He added that the gondola—the basketlike structure suspended beneath the balloon to hold passengers and equipment—would have destroyed one of the homes.

"It's one thing for us to risk our necks in the balloon," Abruzzo added. "But the thing you don't do is risk any injury to anybody on the ground."

To slow the descent of the balloon, all remaining ballast was dropped from it. "Then we were caught in a whirling spin, and the rate of ascent went to 1,500 feet a minute, the most rapid I ever saw for a helium balloon," Abruzzo said.

After rising, the balloonists were in darkness in the storm again. The balloon reached 6,000 feet, not enough to cross the 8,000-foot mountain peaks ahead. It passed a ridge, and they then decided to make their landing on the other side. They put down the drag ropes—heavy ropes that are thrown out of the balloon just before landing to lighten the load and break the fall. The balloon slowed and the crew saw the mountainside coming up.

The men knew that if they took the balloon up again, there would be no way to stop. So they got ready, and when the gondola touched the ground, Abruzzo fired the separation charge, which deflates the balloon so the wind will not drag the gondola. "The balloon exploded," he said, "and we all ended up in one end of the gondola."

The balloonists landed near Covelo, California. They notified searchers that they were safe for the night, and then, Abruzzo said, he went to sleep for "the best night's sleep since we left Japan," 84 hours and 31 minutes earlier, on the longest balloon ride ever made.

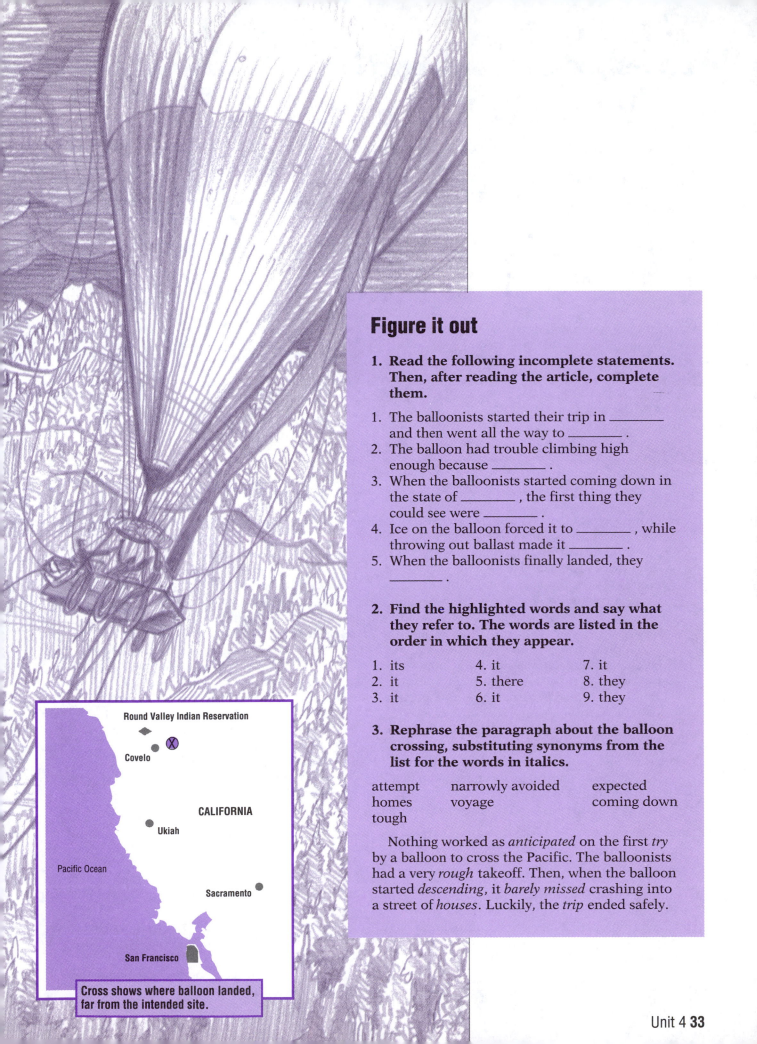

Figure it out

1. **Read the following incomplete statements. Then, after reading the article, complete them.**

   1. The balloonists started their trip in _____ and then went all the way to _____ .
   2. The balloon had trouble climbing high enough because _____ .
   3. When the balloonists started coming down in the state of _____ , the first thing they could see were _____ .
   4. Ice on the balloon forced it to _____ , while throwing out ballast made it _____ .
   5. When the balloonists finally landed, they _____ .

2. **Find the highlighted words and say what they refer to. The words are listed in the order in which they appear.**

1. its	4. it	7. it
2. it	5. there	8. they
3. it	6. it	9. they

3. **Rephrase the paragraph about the balloon crossing, substituting synonyms from the list for the words in italics.**

attempt	narrowly avoided	expected
homes	voyage	coming down
tough		

   Nothing worked as *anticipated* on the first *try* by a balloon to cross the Pacific. The balloonists had a very *rough* takeoff. Then, when the balloon started *descending*, it *barely missed* crashing into a street of *houses*. Luckily, the *trip* ended safely.

Round Valley Indian Reservation

Covelo

CALIFORNIA

Ukiah

Pacific Ocean

Sacramento

San Francisco

Cross shows where balloon landed, far from the intended site.

17. So, what comes next?

1. **Tell your partner how to do one of the following:**

1. Start a car, back it out of a driveway, and drive forward.
2. Change a flat tire on a busy highway.
3. Play a game or sport popular in your country.
4. Make your favorite recipe or national dish.

Hector Cantor, an amateur pilot, is explaining some of the basics of flying to one of his friends, Ned Lee.

Listen to the conversation.

2

Ned Tell me something . . . aren't you ever afraid?

Hector Never. I can't wait to get up there.

Ned I've always wondered what it's like—flying your own plane. I mean, what do you do exactly?

Hector Well, before even getting into the airplane, you have to make the preflight inspection. You have to check things like the propeller, the wings, the tires, the fuel tanks . . .

Ned Yeah, I guess that would be important.

Hector Yes, it's *extremely* important. In fact, a few times while making the inspection, I discovered some real problems.

Ned Better than discovering them in the air! So, what comes next?

Hector Then, you start the engine and contact ground control for permission to taxi onto the runway.

Ned And after that you're ready for takeoff?

Hector Not quite so fast. Next, you have to check all of the instruments and controls in the cockpit, as well as some of the other parts of the plane—like the engines while they're running, the wing flaps, the tail rudder . . .

Ned I never knew it was so complicated! Is that it?

Hector Yes. Finally, you're ready to fly. So you contact the control tower and ask for permission to take off.

Ned What about once you're in the air?

Hector Well, you always have to keep your eyes on the instruments and look around for other aircraft when flying.

Ned Hmm . . . it sounds a little bit like driving a car. In fact, I think I'll stick to that—it's closer to the ground!

3. **Match.**

1. Before getting into the plane,
2. After making the preflight inspection,
3. After getting permission to taxi onto the runway,
4. Once you've checked the instruments and controls in the cockpit,
5. When flying,

a. you start the engine and contact ground control.
b. you're ready to fly.
c. you always have to look around for other aircraft.
d. you check the propeller, the wings, the tires, and the fuel tanks.
e. you have to check all of the instruments and controls in the cockpit.

18. The first thing you should do is...

1 ▶ Listen to the flight attendant tell the passengers how to use oxygen masks in an emergency. Number the pictures in the correct order.

2 ▶ Using the illustrations below, play the role of a first-aid instructor and tell your partner what to do in an emergency. Order your instructions by using some of the expressions in the box.

First . . .	Last . . .
Then . . .	Finally . . .
Next . . .	

If you need to give artificial respiration, do the following:

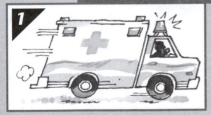

1 Have someone call an ambulance.

2 Place the victim on his/her back with the victim's face to the side.

3 Open the victim's mouth and clear it of any foreign objects.

4 Tilt the victim's head back and check to be sure his/her tongue is in its natural position—if not, pull it back from the back of the throat.

5 Pinch the victim's nose and take a deep breath.

6 Blow into the mouth until the victim's lungs expand. Repeat, one breath every 5 seconds.

3 ▶ **Study the frames: Using time markers to put events in order**

First,	you have to make the preflight inspection.
Then,	you start the engine.
Next,	you contact ground control.
Last,	you check the instruments.
Finally,	you're ready to fly.

You may substitute *after that* for *then*, *next*, or *last*.
First, you have to make the inspection.
After that, you start the engine.

Once **As soon as**	you've started the engine, continue your checking.
By then, **By that time,**	you're almost ready to fly.
By the time you've finished,	you're ready to fly.

The meaning of *once* is less immediate than *as soon as*.
I'll call Jim *once* I get home. = I'll call him sometime after I get home.
I'll call him *as soon as* I get home. = I'll call him right after I walk in the door.

4 ▶ **Victoria found this note from her mother when she got up Saturday morning. Rewrite the note, completing the sentences with appropriate time markers. Most items have more than one answer.**

Victoria,

I need you to help me today. I have to work until 12:00 and I forgot to tell you before you went to bed last night.

_____, please strip your bed and throw the sheets in the washing machine. The machine is all set for you. Just add 1/4 cup of detergent and close the lid.

_____, Toby needs a bath. The dog shampoo is under the kitchen sink, and there's an old towel on the kitchen counter. _____, brush him well; _____, give him his bath. _____ you've finished, let him go outside so he can run around and dry in the sun.

_____ you're done washing Toby (and cleaning the bathtub), your sheets should be done. Put them in the dryer and set the timer for 1/2 hour.

_____, I should be home.

Love,
Mom

5 ▸ Study the frame:
General statements
with *before*, *after*,
and *when*

Before	you get getting	in the plane,	you do the preflight inspection.
After	you start starting	the engine,	you contact ground control.
When	you fly flying	an airplane,	you should be careful.

While is not used very often to make general statements.

6 ▸ Listen to the conversation.
▸ Act out similar conversations in small groups. Find out what hobbies or special interests the members of your group have. Ask a group member to explain how something is done.

A Do you have any hobbies?
B Well, I make pottery.
C Can you tell us a little bit about how you do it?
B Well, first, you take a piece of clay and center it in the middle of a potter's wheel. Then, while the wheel is turning, you shape the clay with your hands. After shaping the clay into a bowl or vase or whatever, you let it dry.
A Is that all? It must be more complicated than that!
B Well, you can decorate the pottery and put a glaze on it. A glaze gives it color and makes it shiny. But before doing this, you have to put the pottery in a very hot oven called a kiln for several hours. This step is called "firing." After firing, you put on the glaze, and then you put the pottery back in the kiln. When the pottery comes out, it's ready to use.

7 ▸ Study the frame:
Specific statements
with *before*, *after*,
when, and *while*

Before	I became becoming	a pilot,	I was a bus driver.
After	I took taking	flying lessons,	I bought a plane.
When	I graduated	from school,	I left home.
While	I was going going	to school,	I worked at an airport.

When talking about something specific, you should express the subject after *when*.

8 ▸ Listen to the conversation.
▸ Act out a similar conversation with a partner. Ask your partner how he or she became interested in the activity he or she explained in exercise 6.

A Pottery sounds like a fun hobby. How did you get interested in it?
B Oh, I don't know. I've always been interested in arts and crafts. Before taking pottery classes, I used to make things out of leather—mostly wallets and belts. Then one day, while looking around at a crafts fair, I got into a conversation with a professional potter. He convinced me to take one of his classes . . . .

19. Your turn

Look at the pictures, and then try to find out how to do at least one of these activities. Bring your notes to class and, working in groups, share your instructions with your classmates. They will ask you questions when they don't understand.

🔊 Listen in

Look carefully at the recipe below. Then listen to an interview in which the well-known chef, Martine Beck, explains how to make her dish, "Adam's Apple." You may wish to take notes while you listen. Then complete the recipe.

Adam's Apple

_____ large _____ , peeled and sliced

_____ tablespoons water

1/4 cup _____

_____ teaspoon cinnamon

_____ cup butter

1/2 cup _____

_____ eggs

_____ cup flour

_____ teaspoon baking powder

_____ , preheat your oven to 350° and butter a 2-quart baking dish.

_____ you are waiting for the oven to heat, combine the apples, the water, the 1/4 cup of sugar, and the cinnamon.

_____ , pour the apple mixture into the baking dish and set it aside.

_____ preparing the apples, in another bowl, mix the butter and the 1/2 cup of sugar until the mixture is fluffy.

_____ , add the eggs and beat well.

_____ , add the flour and baking powder and mix well.

_____ , spread the batter over the apples and bake in the oven for 50 minutes.

_____ the dish is ready, serve it hot with vanilla ice cream on the side. It serves 4 to 6 people.

20. On your own

1. Choose one of the options below.

1. Write the instructions for making your favorite recipe. If you need help, ask a friend or a member of your family.
2. Write about yourself, explaining how you got to your current position in life. First tell what you are doing and then explain how your past experiences led you to this point.

2. Choose one of the pictures and write the instructions.

How to play a videotape.

How to send a fax.

How to make a glass of fresh orange juice.

How to wash clothes.

PREVIEW

FUNCTIONS/THEMES	LANGUAGE	FORMS
Describe something Talk about dimensions	What are they like? They were much bigger and heavier than the ones we have today. It's four feet wide and six feet long. Your dining area is only eight feet by eight feet.	
Make comparisons	How much did the old glass milk bottles weigh? They weighed about 14 ounces more than today's paper milk cartons.	Dimensions and weight
Describe a household problem	The linoleum looks so dull and worn. Some of these nice yellow vinyl tiles would make a big difference.	Order of adjectives

Preview the reading.

1. Work with a partner. Wonders are unusually amazing things or events. Tell your partner about ancient wonders in your culture or in a culture you know about. Also tell your partner what you know about the pictures below.

The Aztec calendar

Machu Picchu

2. Before you read the article on pages 42–43, look at the title and the photos on page 42. What do you know about these ancient wonders? Discuss your ideas with a partner.

21. Ancient Wonders

by Murray Rubenstein

The Great Wall of China.

Incan village in Peru.

The Roman aqueduct in Segovia, Spain.

If you stood on the moon and looked back toward Earth, you could see with the naked eye only one structure: the Great Wall of China, which was built in the third century B.C. Today the wall stands as a reminder that modern technology owes a tremendous amount to the accomplishments of ancient builders and engineers. With surprising ingenuity they used the powers of nature to design splendid buildings, bridges, and tunnels. Above all, they passed down to modern engineers their conviction that by hard work the world could be molded and reshaped for the benefit of the people living in it.

By far the best-documented technology of the ancient world was that of the Greeks and Romans. The Greeks had a firm grasp of mathematics and physics, and they used their knowledge to build great buildings, many of which are standing today. The Romans, in turn, applied Greek theory on an even grander scale to build magnificent highways and viaducts, public baths, and elaborate sewage systems. The Romans constructed 56,000 miles of roads and highways; some parts of the Appian Way can still be seen southeast of Rome.

Less well known are the road-building activities of South America's Incas, who flourished during the fifteenth century. The Incas built over 10,000 miles of roads throughout the Andes Mountains, from present-day Argentina to Colombia. Their Royal Road of the Sun, 3,250 miles long, was the longest road in the ancient world—far longer than any Roman road.

The Incas were also great bridge builders. Around the year 1350, they constructed a suspension bridge across the great Apurímac River in the Andes in present-day Peru. The bridge, still in use in 1890, contained neither metal nor wood. Its suspension cables, which were 148 feet long and as thick as a human body, were made by twisting the strong fibers of a local plant.

Yet long before any of these cultures flourished, the ancient Chinese were making the most of their scientific knowledge. The most amazing of all Chinese engineering accomplishments was, of course, the Great Wall. Begun in the third century B.C., the Wall was intended primarily as a defense against invaders from the north. The Great Wall stretches for over 1,400 miles (2,500 miles counting curves) and separates Mongolia from China. Branching off from the main wall are numerous extensions, which were designed to anticipate special military problems. If the Great Wall and all of its branches were set in a straight line, they would extend across the Atlantic Ocean from England to the United States.

The Chinese were actually centuries ahead of the rest of the world in many areas. Around 300 B.C. they developed the world's oldest system of roads. The national highway system was carefully maintained, and drivers of horse-drawn wagons caught speeding were arrested and fined.

Regularly during the Middle Ages and Renaissance, Europe became excited over "inventions" that had originated in China centuries earlier and had migrated slowly westward to Europe. Canals and rivers were controlled by locks in China in the third century B.C., seventeen centuries ahead of Europe. When we sit down to have a dish of spaghetti, we are really having a Chinese meal. Spaghetti originated in China, and it was brought back to Italy by Marco Polo. Gunpowder, which finally made its way to Europe in the 1400s, actually originated in China in the eighth century. The Chinese even developed the process of printing with wood or metal blocks in 600 A.D., over 800 years before Johann Gutenberg printed the famous Gutenberg bible, the first book to be printed in movable type in Europe.

When we look at the incredible accomplishments of the Chinese, it becomes clear that the Greeks and Romans could have done more with their technology. Perhaps one reason they didn't is that they felt no need for machines. Slaves provided the ultimate cheap labor.

It is likely that 2,000 years from today people will look back on us with a mixture of admiration and puzzlement. Just as we do when we look back on ancient civilizations, future people will marvel at our ingenuity under such primitive conditions. But just as we wonder why the Greeks and Romans failed to develop their science further, people of the future will no doubt shake their heads in puzzlement over our failure to make even better use of our scientific knowledge.

Figure it out

1. **Before reading the entire article, scan the first sentence of each paragraph to find out which ancient cultures the article focuses on. Then read the last paragraph and summarize the article's main point.**

2. **As you read the article, pay attention to the important points that are made about each culture. When you have finished, complete the sentences below with the name of the correct people(s) or place(s). Then find several facts in the article that support each statement.**

   1. Although they were not that well known, the _____ built an incredible system of roads and an amazing bridge.
   2. The _____ made full use of their scientific knowledge. Many inventions originated in _____ centuries before they reached _____ .
   3. The accomplishments of the _____ in building were very impressive; however, they could have done more with their technology.

3. **Many modifiers of nouns may be formed by combining a noun or adverb with the past participle of a verb, as in these examples from the article:**

   - **horse-drawn wagons =** *wagons* that are/were *drawn* by *horses*

   - **the best-documented technology = the** *technology* that is/was *documented the best*

   Rephrase the sentences below, using noun modifiers.

   1. I bought a beautiful chair yesterday that was made by hand. (The modifier is one word.)
   2. I would never take a job at Lou's Bookstore. The clerks that are paid the highest only make $20,000 a year.
   3. It's important to study hard. Only the students that are prepared the best get into good universities.
   4. This is a watch that's operated by batteries. You'll never have to wind it.

22. It belonged to your grandparents.

1. People didn't always travel by car or plane, turn on the water faucet for a drink of water, go to the supermarket for a package of flour, or watch TV for entertainment. What important changes in technology have taken place during your own lifetime or during your parents' lifetime? Describe at least one change to your partner.

 Lisa Scott is helping her parents clean out the attic when she finds something unexpected.

Listen to the conversation.

②

Lisa	Hey, look what I found! What is this ugly old thing? It weighs a ton.
Mrs. Scott	Hold on now. . . . That happens to be a radio, and I used to listen to it when I was just a kid. It belonged to your grandparents.
Lisa	It's incredible! Why would anyone have wanted a radio that looked like this?
Mr. Scott	Well, first of all, there weren't any smaller ones in those days. Furthermore, this radio was considered quite attractive when my mother and father were young.
Lisa	Really? Hmm . . .
Mr. Scott	You know, in those days people would invite their friends over to listen to the radio for the evening.
Lisa	No kidding!
Mrs. Scott	Remember when the first transistor radios came out, Jim? They caused as much excitement as laptop computers.
Mr. Scott	That's the truth. I remember getting a shiny, new silver radio for my birthday. I couldn't believe it was only six inches long and I was able to carry it around in my pocket.
Mrs. Scott	It's not only appliances that have gotten smaller, though. Think of houses, apartments, and cars. Even ceilings used to be several feet higher than those in modern houses.
Mr. Scott	Not to mention doorways! Now if you're over six feet tall, you have to bend over.
Lisa	How tall are you exactly?
Mr. Scott	Six two, unfortunately. (*Rubs bump on head*)

3. Find another way to say it.

1. It fit in my pocket.
2. It was only six inches in length.
3. What's your exact height?
4. That's true.
5. You couldn't find any smaller ones then.
6. It's really heavy!
7. People thought this radio was very good-looking.

23. What were they like?

1 ▶ Listen to people describe some old-fashioned items. Number the items in the order of the conversations you hear.

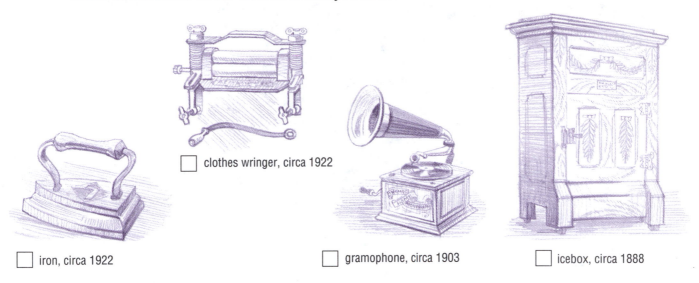

☐ clothes wringer, circa 1922

☐ iron, circa 1922

☐ gramophone, circa 1903

☐ icebox, circa 1888

2 ▶ Listen to the conversation.
▶ Act out similar conversations with a partner. You would like to buy the items in the ad for your house or apartment. Your partner will help you figure out if you can use each one.

A I saw an ad for a beautiful old pine table. I'm thinking of buying it.
B Really? Where would you put it?
A I thought I'd put it in the dining area.
B Well, will it fit? How big is it?
A It's four feet wide and six feet long.
B I think it would be too long. Your dining area is only eight feet by eight feet.

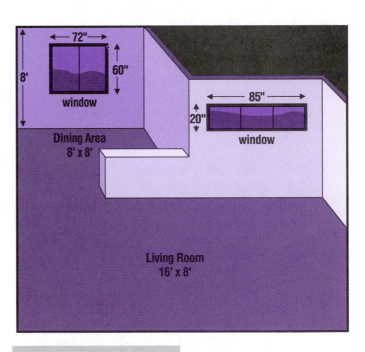

Beautiful old pine table, 4' wide x 6' long. Reasonable price. Call 555-4043.

Pair of floor-length red Japanese curtains. 100% silk. 72" wide x 90" long. $35. Call Marion at 555-9756.

Antique Swiss grandfather clock, 7½ feet tall. 555-7566 after 6 P.M.

Large, sturdy oak bookcase, 7' wide x 8' high x 1' deep. Deep enough for those annoying big books. Must sell. Only $125. Call 555-4321.

4' × 6' = 4 feet by 6 feet
89" = 89 inches

3 ► **Study the frames: Dimensions and weight**

How			He's		
	tall	is Tom?	He's	**six feet**	**tall**.
	high	is the ceiling?		**eight feet**	**high**.
	wide	is the material?		**two yards**	**wide**.
How	**long**	is the trail?	It's	**three miles**	**long**.
	thick	is the steak?		**an inch**	**thick**.
	deep	is the bookcase?		**one foot**	**deep**.

Singular	Plural
foot	feet

Some opposites

tall	short
high	low
wide	narrow
long	short
thick	thin
deep	shallow
heavy	light

How	**big**	is your living room?	It's	**12 feet by 14 feet**.

How	**heavy**	is the box?	It's It weighs	**ten pounds**.
How much	does the box **weigh**?			

Comparisons of dimensions

The bookcase is	two feet ten pounds	**higher heavier**	**than**	the desk.
The bookcase weighs	ten pounds	**more**	**than**	the desk.

Always use the word *tall* when talking about a person's height. When talking about an object, generally use the word *high*. *Clock* is one exception.

4 ► **Write a question and answer for each item. Then act out the conversations with a partner.**

1. The old glass milk bottles weighed 15 ounces. Today's paper milk cartons weigh 1 ounce.
   A *How much did the old glass milk bottles weigh?*
   B *15 ounces. They weighed about 14 ounces more than today's paper milk cartons.*

2. Ceilings in old apartments were often 10 feet high. Today's ceilings are 8 feet high.

3. The first pocket calculators weighed about 14 ounces. The new ones weigh less than 2 ounces.

4. The average woman in the eighteenth century was under 5 feet tall.
   The average woman today is about 5 feet 5 inches tall.

5. The first television screens were only 10 inches wide. Now some television screens are 36 inches wide.

6. When computers were first developed, they were 10 feet high by 10 feet wide.
   Today some laptop computers are only 10 inches tall and less than 1 foot wide.

5 ▶ Listen to the conversation.
   ▶ Act out similar conversations with a partner, using the information
     in the box and the solutions suggested by the pictures.

A I really ought to do something about my kitchen floor. The
   linoleum looks so dull and worn.
B Why don't you put down some new tiles?
A You know, that's a good idea. Some of these nice yellow
   vinyl tiles would make a big difference.

Some problems
a dull, worn linoleum floor
peeling paint on the bathroom walls
piles of books cluttering up the floor

6 ▶ Study the frame: Order of adjectives

	Ordinal number	Cardinal number	General	Age	Color	Material	Origin	Noun
	first	**two**					**Japanese**	movies
the			ugly,	old	black			dress
			large		blue	cotton		pants
			shiny,	new		leather		boots

▲

This category includes adjectives of opinion, size, shape, cost, and condition. Their order is generally flexible.

Use a comma between adjectives if the comma could be replaced by *and*.
   the charming, intelligent professor =
   the charming and intelligent professor

7 ▶ Rewrite the letter, completing the sentences by putting the adjectives in parentheses in the correct order.

Dear Charles,   August 14
   I'm having a wonderful time sightseeing in Italy. I've especially
enjoyed the _____ (fascinating, Roman, old) ruins. You know I've
always been interested in history.
   I've also done some shopping. I went to a _____ (Italian, little)
antique shop over the weekend, and I bought _____ (beautiful,
turn-of-the-century, several) things I think you'll like. I bought a
_____ (Italian, hand-painted) mandolin and a _____ (green,
small, porcelain) vase. I also bought a _____ (rosewood, square)
table, which will look great in our apartment.
   See you soon.

                                                    Love,
                                                    Mona

24. Your turn

How does the photo of New York 100 years ago compare with the photo of New York today? What do you think will be different about big cities by the year 2500? Discuss these questions in small groups. Then work together to design an ideal "city of the future."

New York City 100 years ago

New York City today

▣ Listen in

A group of people at a museum are listening to a museum guide. Read the questions below. Then listen to the conversation and answer the questions.

1. Which kitchen in the photos did the guide describe?

2. What explanations did members of the group give for features of this kitchen? Choose *a* or *b*.
   1. The ceiling was high so
      a. smoke and heat from the fireplace could rise.
      b. there could be more space for storage.
   2. A large fireplace was necessary because
      a. all food was prepared at home and many things were cooked at the same time.
      b. families were much larger in those days.
   3. In general, kitchens were larger than they are today because
      a. people needed more space to store supplies and to prepare and cook food.
      b. families spent a lot of their time in the kitchen.

An eighteenth-century Italian kitchen with helpers preparing vegetables, meat, and poultry.

A kitchen in the 1950s.

A modern kitchen, spacious and airy.

Work with a group to discuss the similarities and differences among the kitchens in the photos. Then discuss what you think kitchens will be like in the year 2500.

25. On your own

1. **You've just won the lottery and are planning to do many exciting things. Write a letter to your friend describing exactly what you'll buy and do. Use at least two adjectives in each descriptive sentence. You can continue the letter below or write your own.**

Dear _____

I've just won the lottery! You've no idea how excited I am. Besides taking a trip to visit you, here are some of the other things I want to do:

- I plan to buy two shiny, new cars—one for city driving and one for the country.
- I want to take my mother on a wonderful, long ocean cruise.
- . . .

2. **Write an essay, choosing one of the options below.**

1. Describe something that really impresses you about contemporary living and compare it to the way it was in the past. Some possible topics are entertainment, clothing, transportation, and appliances.

2. Describe something that people in your country used to do (or an item they used to use) that has changed significantly. You may choose a topic you've discussed in this unit or an idea of your own.

PREVIEW

FUNCTIONS/THEMES	LANGUAGE	FORMS
Give reasons Talk about consequences	What were your parents like when you were growing up? They were very strict with me since/as they believed children needed a lot of discipline. One of my brothers was near my age, so we played together a lot.	Connectors (conjunctions and prepositions)
Make a proposal Talk about people	Ms. Abrams, on the other hand, is very friendly and easygoing. Therefore, I think she would make a much better impression on clients. I suggest that we have Ms. Martin and Ms. Abrams switch jobs. I don't get along with my older sister. I try to stand up for myself.	Three-word verbs

Preview the reading.

1. Work in small groups. Your birth rank means the order in which you were born among the children in your family. Tell the members of your group your birth rank. Then guess and discuss how your birth rank has affected your life.

2. Substitute *Firstborn children* or *Later children* for the pronoun *They* in each statement below. Try to guess the answers.

1. They may have trouble making close friends.
2. They like creative fields such as music, art, or writing.
3. They are relaxed and sociable.
4. They like professions such as teaching and politics.
5. They are usually very ambitious.
6. They often make good salespeople.
7. They tend to be somewhat conservative.

BIRTH RANK:

It was probably no accident that George Orwell used the term Big Brother for the dictator in his novel *1984.* Psychologists have long been aware that birth order generally creates certain personality traits.

Big brothers and sisters usually develop leadership tendencies early in life, mainly because of the responsibilities for younger siblings given to them by their parents. The danger, experts on family and child psychology report, is that if the older sibling takes that role to an extreme, he or she can become an overbearing and tyrannical adult.

Studies of nearly 3,000 people conducted by Walter Toman, former professor of psychology at Brandeis University in Massachusetts, have found that, under normal circumstances, firstborns are usually the most strongly motivated toward achievement. This, he maintains, is mainly a result of parental expectations.

This and other research suggests that firstborn children generally become more conservative than their siblings because they receive most of the parental discipline. Used to caring for others, they are more likely to move toward such leadership professions as teaching and politics. Less social and flexible because they became accustomed in the very early years to acting alone, they may have difficulty making close friends.

By contrast, the researchers say, later children are more likely to be more relaxed and sociable, and less inhibited than the eldest child because their parents were more relaxed. However, the later children are often less ambitious and are uncomfortable making decisions for others, and will seek work that fits such needs. This, according to researchers, may help explain why younger siblings tend to favor the creative fields such as music, art, or writing.

Later children often make good salespeople because persuasion may have been the only tool they had to counteract the power of the eldest. Younger children tend to remain forever "the baby," enjoyable to be around, and inspiring compassion; but they can become overdependent on others.

While birth order is clearly only one of the many factors that affect development, its impact should not be underestimated. When people understand how their birth order causes them to react, they do

EFFECTS ON PERSONALITY

by Andrée Brooks

not find change so threatening, says Lucille Forer, a clinical psychologist in Malibu, California, who has written extensively on the subject.

An understanding of birth order can sometimes help a marriage work. Not long ago, Dr. Forer was working with a woman who had become so domineering that her marriage was in trouble. Once she understood her tendencies, Dr. Forer said, she could begin to modify her behavior.

Maida Webster, a family therapist and school consultant in Norwich, Connecticut, recently conducted a workshop called "Birth Order Factor." She told of a husband and wife who complained bitterly about being let down by the other. Neither, it seemed, had taken over the leadership role that each had expected the other to assume. When it was

pointed out that this was probably because each had been a younger sibling, they began to comprehend the problem.

"Is there an ideal combination for marriage?" Mrs. Webster was asked. Both at work and in personal relationships, she said, people seem to get along best when they repeat the patterns of childhood, which means that it helps to marry someone in a complementary position. In contrast, two people who were the eldest children can expect conflict.

"Is there any best position in the birth order?" asked someone else. Mrs. Webster said no, that there were benefits and disadvantages to all. However, she went on, recognizing tendencies can enhance opportunities to make the most of positive traits and minimize negative ones.

Figure it out

1. **Read the article. When you have finished, check your answers to item 2 on page 51. Then, for each statement, find a reason given in the article to explain it.**

2. **Make a list of the personality traits discussed in the article, dividing them, according to the author's opinion, into the four categories listed below. Then, using the information in your lists, explain why it might be best to marry someone whose birth rank is different from your own.**

   1. Firstborn children, advantages
   2. Firstborn children, disadvantages
   3. Later children, advantages
   4. Later children, disadvantages

3. **The prefixes over- and under-, as in overdependent and underestimate, may be placed before many words to mean "more than normal or desired" and "less than normal or desired," respectively. Complete the sentences below with either over- or under- plus the word in parentheses.**

   1. The reason Marcy's son is so _____ (weight) is that he eats constantly. I don't understand why she lets him _____ (eat) so.
   2. My daughter's teacher says she's an _____ (achiever), and that I don't push her enough. That may be, but I want her to enjoy herself.
   3. Tony really _____ (protect) his brother. He never lets him out of his sight.
   4. I'm really _____ (paid) on my job. If I don't get a good raise, I'm going to leave.

27. Look at the bright side.

1. Which of the following words best describes the way you were as a child? Explain to your partner why you think you were that way.

outgoing   friendly
shy   unfriendly

cooperative   self-confident
uncooperative   insecure

 Angela Mendez, a sales representative, is discussing her childhood with a coworker, Nick Andros, at an office party.

Listen to the conversation.

2

Angela   Hi, Nick! How's that boring desk job going these days?

Nick   Boring? I happen to like working at my desk. As a matter of fact, I don't know how you can put up with being a sales representative, Angela. I mean, don't you ever get tired of trying to convince people all the time?

Angela   Actually, that's the part I enjoy most. It reminds me of my childhood.

Nick   How's that?

Angela   Well, I had an older sister, so I quickly learned to stand up for myself and not give in to everything she wanted.

Nick   But what does that have to do with being a sales representative?

Angela   Well, in order to get my way, I had to convince her that my way was right. It took a lot of effort, too. Since she was older, she usually thought she knew better.

Nick   I've heard that older brothers and sisters can be pretty bossy. I wouldn't know. I was an only child.

Angela   My sister was as tough as nails. She never let me get away with anything. She even used to punish me for misbehaving.

Nick   She sounds like a real tyrant!

Angela   Yes, but look at the bright side. As a result, I learned the skills I use now when I deal with my toughest customers. They almost always have a soft side underneath.

Nick   Well, I guess there's always something you can learn from your childhood. . . .

3. Match.

1. I was an only child,
2. Since my parents thought discipline was important,
3. I had to stand up for myself
4. My parents always rewarded me
5. My brother was older than I was,

a. in order to get what I wanted.
b. for getting good grades in school.
c. so I didn't have to share things with anyone else.
d. so he always treated me like a baby.
e. I didn't misbehave very often.

28. How did you get along with them?

1 ► Listen to the conversation.
 ► Act out similar conversations with a partner. Describe what your parents were like when you were a child and give reasons for their behavior.

A What were your parents like when you were growing up?

B My parents? Well, they were very strict with me, since / as they believed children needed a lot of discipline. That's how they had been brought up. How about yours?

A Well, they weren't very strict, but they used to pressure me a lot. Since / As my father loved music, he wanted me to learn to play the piano. He used to get mad at me for not practicing.

My parents . . .	They believed . . .
were strict.	children needed discipline.
were supportive.	children needed encouragement.
were permissive.	children should have fun.
pressured me to study a lot.	education was important.
wanted me to make my own decisions.	children should develop independence.
spent a lot of time with me.	family life was important.

He used to get mad at me *for* not practicing. =
He used to get mad at me because I didn't practice.

2 ► Listen to the two possible conversations.
 ► Act out similar conversations with a partner. Tell your partner whether you had brothers and/or sisters and discuss the consequences of having (or not having) them.

A Do you come from a large family?

B Yes. I have two brothers and three sisters.

A How did you get along with them when you were growing up?

B Well, one of my brothers was near my age, so we played together a lot. My other brother and my sisters were older, and as a result, they were always ordering us around.

B No. I was an only child.

A Did you ever wish you had brothers and sisters?

B Yes. I was the only one my parents had to worry about. Therefore, they expected an awful lot from me.

Some ways to talk about consequences
One of my brothers was near my age, so we played together a lot.
One of my brothers was near my age. As a result, we competed for things. Thus, he always knew what I was doing. Therefore, we had to learn to share.

So is less formal than *as a result*, *thus*, and *therefore*.

3 ► **Study the frames: Connectors (conjunctions and prepositions)**

Connectors that show a reason

She punished me	**because**	I had misbehaved.
	for	misbehaving.
She thought she knew better	**as** **since**	she was older.

More formal	Less formal
as	since
thus therefore as a result	so
in order to so that	to so

Connectors that show a consequence

My sister was older.	**Thus, Therefore, As a result,**	she was always giving me advice.
My sister was older,	**so**	

Connectors that show a purpose

I went to business school	**(in order) to**	study marketing.
	so (that)	I could study marketing.
	for	a degree in marketing.

▲

in order to + base form
so that + sentence

4 ► **Listen to the conversations. Write *R* if the speaker is giving a reason for a childhood event and *C* if the speaker is talking about the consequences of a childhood event.**

5 ► **Find out about something your partner is doing or a decision he or she has made. Then ask for an explanation.**

A *Why are you studying English?*
B *(I'm studying it) in order to get a job with an international company.*

Ask someone why he or she . . .

is studying _____ .
is going back to _____ .
decided to be a(n) _____ .
took a trip to _____ .
moved into his or her own
  apartment.

Some reasons

(in order) to get a job
(in order) to be closer to my family
so (that) I could work abroad
so (that) I could learn about the culture
for the peace and quiet

6 ► Rewrite the memo, completing the sentences with appropriate connectors. Some items have more than one answer.

> **TO:** Caroline MacGregor, President
> **FROM:** Marcel Jacobi, Office Manager
> **SUBJECT:** Personnel reassignment
>
> About a month ago, both our receptionist and our secretary left the company on short notice. _____ , I had to hire their replacements, Andrea Martin and Judy Abrams, rather quickly. Ms. Martin had worked as a receptionist before, _____ I made her the receptionist. _____ both employees are new, I have been watching their work closely. I am writing this memo _____ give you the results of my observations.
>
> Ms. Martin is a conscientious worker, but she is not very friendly on the job. I have had to call her into my office several times _____ being rude to clients. Ms. Abrams, on the other hand, is very friendly and easygoing. _____ , I think she would make a much better impression on clients. I suggest that we have Ms. Martin and Ms. Abrams switch jobs.
>
> I would appreciate a quick response from you _____ I can make this change as soon as possible.
>
> Thank you.

7 ► Study the frames:
Three-word verbs

I don't	**get along with**	my older sister.
I'm tired of	**putting up with**	the way she treats me.

I refuse to	**give in to**	her.
I try to	**stand up for**	myself.

Some other three-word verbs

My daughter, Mary, **is up to** no good. She **gets away with** anything she wants. She **looks up to** the wrong people and **goes along with** whatever they do. Last week her teacher **walked in on** her while she was smoking in the girls' room. She told me to **check up on** Mary more closely and **find out about** her activities.

I want her to **keep out of** trouble. I made her **cut down on** parties during the week, but she still **ends up with** bad grades. She doesn't **keep up with** her schoolwork, and she can't **come up with** the answers on tests. She always tries to **get out of** work and **looks down on** kids who study.

I'm starting to **run out of** patience. She's always one step ahead of me, and I just can't seem to **catch up with** her. But someday she'll **be in for** a big surprise.

8 ► Rewrite the interview with the famous burglar Eric Sheridan in his prison cell, completing the sentences with appropriate three-word verbs from exercise 7.

Q: What do you suppose led you to a life of crime, Mr. Sheridan?
A: Who knows? As a kid I _____ some kind of mischief twenty-four hours a day. And I was always trying to _____ work. Maybe I'm just lazy.

Q: So your parents let you _____ your bad behavior?
A: Oh, no! My father never _____ anything! That's why I left home.

Q: Did you ever think you'd _____ a twenty-five-year jail sentence?
A: No, I never thought I'd get caught. I thought I was too smart.

Q: How *did* the police finally _____ you?
A: Well, it was late at night and I was in this fancy house—Lady Waverly's house. I was almost sure no one was home, but as it turned out, I _____ a big surprise. Just as I was opening up Lady Waverly's jewelry box, she _____ me. And believe it or not, she had a black belt in karate!

Q: Well, it looks as if you have a long vacation ahead of you, Mr. Sheridan.
A: Oh, no, I haven't _____ tricks yet. I'll be out of prison a lot sooner than you think.

29. Your turn

Look at these pictures of different families. Then, working in groups, describe and compare the home life of the families. Discuss the questions below, and give reasons for your opinions. Say whether your opinions are based on your own childhood experiences or on those of people you know.

1. What are some of the advantages and disadvantages of each family situation?
2. How do you think the children in each family get along with each other and with other people as a result of their family life?
3. How do you think the family life of these children will affect their lives as adults?

the Alvarez family
Ramon
Anita
Luisa
Cecilia

the Patterson family
Shirley
Susan
Sandra
Evan
Maureen
Donald

the Gibson family
Billy
Kathleen
Clare
Colleen
Terry
Heather
Kevin
Gwen

the Stevens family

Gordon

Nora

Megan

the Ono family

Nobuo

Yoshio

Teruo

Akira

the Simek family

Florence

Roger

Joanna

Listen in

Dr. Dorne and Dr. Saporta, two child psychologists, are being interviewed on a radio talk show. Read the statements below and the questions that follow them. Then listen to a part of the interview and answer the questions.

a. Only children show higher achievement than children from very large families.
b. The size of a family has nothing to do with the development of the children in it.
c. Children with many brothers and sisters have more people to teach them how to get along with others and how to solve their problems.

1. Which two of the three viewpoints were expressed in the discussion?
2. Who expressed each viewpoint, Dr. Dorne or Dr. Saporta?

30. On your own

1. You write an advice column for young people. Answer the letter.

> I'm having a hard time getting along with my older sister. She's always bossing me around and telling me what to do. I know that most of the time she means well, but the way she treats me bothers me. For example, yesterday she came into my room without knocking and said "Get some air in this place. Open a window or two. And you're not sitting at your desk properly. Don't slouch; sit up!" Then she went over and opened a window and came over and made me sit up at my desk. I could have screamed! What should I do?
>
> Frustrated

2. Choose one of the options below.

1. You are a teacher and one of the children in the pictures in Lesson 29 is in your class. The child has a problem with a brother or sister and is doing poorly in school as a result. Write a report to the principal, explaining the problem and its causes. Make a recommendation.

2. You are a family counselor and you have to give a speech on sibling relationships to a group of parents. Write a speech in which you discuss the importance of sibling relationships in personality development, and the consequences of growing up with brothers and/or sisters as opposed to growing up alone.

3. Write a short article on different ways of raising children. Include some different ideas on how to raise children; some opinions on how you personally think children should be raised, and why you think so; and some experiences from your own childhood that support your opinions.

Review of units 1-6

1 ▶ Before you read the article on insomnia—difficulty falling or staying asleep—try to answer these questions. When you have finished reading, compare your answers with the information in the article and make any necessary corrections.

1. What are some things that can cause a sleepless night?
2. What should someone with insomnia do about it? What should he or she not do?
3. Have you ever had insomnia or do you know of anyone who has? What did you or that person do about it?

Laying Insomnia to Rest
by Susan Gilbert

When the task at hand is to get a good night's sleep, trying hard is not the way to succeed. Twisting and turning in search of a comfortable position in bed makes your body do the opposite of what it's supposed to do at night. Instead of slowing down, your heartbeat races. Instead of relaxing, your leg muscles twitch. You watch the clock and wonder what you're doing wrong.

Over ten million people in the United States alone are seeking medical help for chronic insomnia—difficulty in falling asleep or staying asleep. For years it has been called a symptom of a number of psychological problems, such as depression, that somehow alter the body's sleep pattern. Now sleep specialists are saying that "bad habits" can have the same effect. These include too little daytime activity and, ironically, its opposite, too much exercise.

"Insomniacs usually begin losing sleep over some problem, such as a death in the family," says psychiatrist Robert Watson, director of the Sleep Disorder Center affiliated with Yale University in Connecticut. "But unlike other people," he adds, "they continue to have trouble sleeping—for months, even years." According to Joyce and Anthony Kales, two psychiatrists at Penn State University in Pennsylvania, insomniacs present a consistent personality profile, as outlined in the November American Journal of Psychiatry. They take things hard, feel they haven't lived "the right kind of life," and are nervous and tense.

Insomniacs share another trait, says psychiatrist Thomas Coates of the University of California, San Francisco: They spend an excessive amount of time thinking about sleep. Contrary to the image of bad sleepers as workaholics, Coates's study indicates that insomniacs spend more time relaxing than others do. He thinks their relative inactivity during the day may alter the body's "clock." Instead of signaling the brain to slow down at night, the clock calls for more activity.

Sleeping late on weekends can also disrupt your body's clock. This is the first bad habit Robert Watson makes patients change at the Sleep Disorders Center. He tells them to rise at the same time each day, even after a night of poor sleep. "After a while," he says, "sleep improves."

Even though it tires you out, exercise won't guarantee a sound sleep. If it is too strenuous, especially just before bedtime, it can drive your pulse too high, causing a restless night. Joyce and Anthony Kales use moderate afternoon exercise, along with methods such as psychotherapy and biofeedback, to treat severe insomniacs.

What is the best thing to do on occasional sleepless nights? Forget sleeping pills. They can actually cause insomnia after three days, by altering the brain's chemistry. Watson recommends drinking milk or eating cheese or tuna, because they are rich in natural sleep-producing aids.

There's something to the old-fashioned remedy of drinking warm milk before bedtime, Watson says. Warming it won't make any difference, but it will help you relax.

2 ▶ Rewrite the paragraphs on insomnia, completing the sentences with appropriate connectors from the box. Some items have more than one answer.

To show a consequence	To show a reason	To show a purpose
thus	because	(in order) to
therefore	for	so (that)
as a result	as	for
so	since	

_____ so many people suffer from insomnia, many doctors have begun to study sleep disorders seriously. Their findings show that many insomniacs can't sleep _____ they have one or more "bad habits."

Some people do strenuous exercise before bedtime _____ they can get a good night's sleep. Many others try to spend a lot of time relaxing _____ the same reason. Still others sleep late on weekends _____ catch up on lost sleep. The sleep specialists say that these "bad habits" actually alter the body's normal processes. _____ , they make the problem even worse.

3 ► Rewrite this letter to a doctor who is a sleep specialist, completing the sentences with appropriate connectors from exercise 2. Some items have more than one answer.

Dear Dr. Mehta,

_____ I'm having so much trouble falling asleep at night, I decided to write to you for your advice. _____ you can get a better idea of my problem, let me tell you a little about myself.

I'm employed full time, but _____ my job as a bookkeeper doesn't pay very well, I'm also studying at night _____ a degree in business. In addition, I have three teenage children to cook, clean, and wash for, _____ I actually have another full-time job at home. _____ , I always get to bed very late, and although I'm exhausted, I can never fall asleep.

A few months ago, I started taking sleeping pills. That was my little secret _____ getting a good night's sleep, but lately the pills haven't been working. Maybe I should take two pills instead of one. I don't know what to do _____ get the rest I need, and I am hoping you can help me.

Sincerely,

Lilly Wolff

Lilly Wolff

4 ► Mrs. Wolff made an appointment with Dr. Mehta. Restate the conversation, combining Dr. Mehta's responses in brackets [ ] into one sentence.

Mrs. Wolff I'm so tired. What can I do?
Dr. Mehta [You need to get enough rest. It's essential.]

Mrs. Wolff *I'm so tired. What can I do?*
Dr. Mehta *It's essential that you get enough rest.*

Mrs. Wolff That's why I've been taking sleeping pills.
Dr. Mehta [You should stop depending on medication for sleep. I recommend that.]
Mrs. Wolff But . . .
Dr. Mehta [People have to simplify their lives in order to get a good night's sleep. Sometimes it's necessary.]
Mrs. Wolff But there's so much I have to take care of.
Dr. Mehta The solution to your problem is your three children. [They should take over a good part of the housework. I seriously suggest this.] [They must do their fair share. You must insist.] [They need to begin to assume some of the responsibility for their own lives. At their age it is also important.]
Mrs. Wolff Yes, I guess they are old enough to take care of themselves.

5 ► What problems does Ming have? What does Vincent suggest as solutions? Read the statements below. Then listen to the conversation and say *Right* or *Wrong* for each item.

Ming's problems
1. She is exhausted.
2. She doesn't like her job.
3. She doesn't like her assistant.
4. She has too much work to do.
5. She doesn't think Vincent understands her.

Vincent's solutions
1. He thinks Ming should talk to her boss.
2. He thinks Ming should work overtime more.
3. He thinks Ming should stop working overtime.
4. He thinks Ming should quit her job.
5. He thinks Ming should take better care of herself.

6 ▶ **As you read the article, try to remember in what order the different steps are done. When you have finished the reading, put the steps below in order.**

___ Once the broken glass has been removed, clean out the old, dried putty from the frame.

___ When the glass is in place, fasten it with glazing points.

___ Then loosen the broken glass with a hammer.

___ Next paint the putty.

___ Then place the new glass in the frame.

___ Before you place the glass in the frame, apply a thin layer of putty to the inside of the frame.

___ After the glass has been secured, apply putty along the frame edge.

___ First place the window frame on a flat surface.

___ As soon as the paint is dry, clean the glass inside and out.

___ After the old, dried putty has been removed, apply a thin coat of paint to the inside of the frame.

7 ▶ **While he was fixing a broken window, Andy cut his wrist badly and his brother had to apply a tourniquet. Read the instructions on applying a tourniquet and complete the sentences with appropriate time markers from the box. Some items have more than one answer.**

first	finally	before
then	once	after
next	as soon as	when
last	by then	

In case of a serious cut, always apply a tourniquet _____ you do anything else. Don't wait for an ambulance because _____ the injured person might have already lost too much blood.

To apply a tourniquet, _____ place a wide cloth close to the wound. _____ , wrap the cloth around the arm or leg and tie a half knot. _____ , place a stick on top of the knot and tie a square knot. _____ you've done that, twist the stick. _____ the bleeding stops, tie the stick in place. _____ you've secured the tourniquet, go to the hospital immediately.

Replacing a Broken Windowpane

When window glass or panes get broken, you can save money and avoid a repair bill if you know how to install the new glass yourself.

MATERIALS
The materials needed for replacing a broken windowpane are putty, glazing points, a small amount of thin paint, and a piece of new glass.

TOOLS
The tools required are a hammer, a pair of pliers, a screwdriver, a putty knife, and a paintbrush.

> **putty:** a thick waterproof mixture used in fitting glass
> **putty knife:** a wide, flat knife used to apply putty
> **glazing points:** small three-cornered pieces of metal used to hold glass in place

REPLACING BROKEN GLASS

1. Place the window frame on a worktable or flat surface with the side showing the old putty facing up.
2. Loosen the broken glass by tapping it lightly with a hammer. Remove the broken pieces from the frame with a pair of pliers. (Wear gloves so you don't cut your hands and goggles to protect your eyes.)
3. Clean out the old, dried putty with a screwdriver or putty knife (Figure 1).
4. Apply a coat of thin paint to the inside of the frame where the glass fits. This will help the putty last longer.
5. Use a putty knife to apply a thin layer of putty to the inside of the frame.
6. Place the glass in the frame. Make sure it's in place properly so it won't break. Press the glass firmly in order to smooth out and seal the putty.
7. To make the glass fit tightly, secure it by driving glazing points into the frame on top of the glass every 5 or 6 inches (Figure 2). Drive these three-cornered points in gently with a screwdriver. Drive them only deep enough to keep the glass in place.
8. Apply putty along the frame edge to cover the glazing points and seal in the glass (Figure 3).
9. Paint the frame after the putty is dry.
10. Clean the glass inside and out with a good window cleaner after the paint is dry.

Figure 1.
Broken glass and old putty are removed from a window frame.

Figure 2.
The new piece of glass is secured with glazing points.

Figure 3.
Putty is applied with a putty knife to seal in the new glass.

8 ▶ You are at a yard sale with a friend who would like to buy the items discussed below for his or her apartment. Develop a conversation for each item, using the first sentence and the information about dimensions below it.

1. I'd like to get that stained glass to put in my hall window.
   stained glass = 64 inches high
   hall window = 66 inches high
   A *I'd like to get that stained glass to put in my hall window.*
   B *How high is your hall window?*
   A *It's 66 inches high.*
   B *Then I don't think the glass would fit. It's two inches shorter than your window.*

2. This window box would look nice full of flowers on my kitchen windowsill.
   window box = 4 feet wide
   windowsill = 2½ feet wide

3. I could use that table to put my television on.
   table = 22 inches wide
   television = 26 inches wide

4. I think this rug would look better in the living room than the one we have now.
   rug = 14 feet long
   length of floor = 12 feet long

5. I'd really like to put this mirror up beside the door.
   mirror = 18 inches wide
   space beside the door = 15 inches wide

9 ▶ Complete the sentences by choosing an appropriate item from the box and putting the adjectives in the correct order.

1. My mother likes antiques. She'd probably love these _____ .
2. Our kitchen needs fixing up. It could really use some of this _____ .
3. My sofa and chairs are falling apart. I'd like to buy some _____ .
4. Ursula wants to get a pet. I think she'd love this _____ .
5. I have a long, narrow hall in my apartment. I'd like to find a _____ .

> kitten: Siamese/white/little
> rug: blue/long/Turkish
> cooking pots: black/iron/old
> living room chairs: brown/leather/new
> wallpaper: yellow/washable

10 ▶ Complete the conversation with the correct forms of the two-word verbs in the box and the direct objects in parentheses.

> call up   think about
> look for   run into
> take back   worry about

A I want to redecorate my living room.
B Really? Have you decided what colors to use?
A Well, not definitely. I _____ (beige walls and light blue furniture). But I can't decide what kind of rug to get.
B I think you should _____ (rug) that has beige and blue in it.
A I _____ (expensive purchases) like that. I'm afraid I won't be able to _____ (it) if I decide I don't like it.
B Why don't you _____ (a few carpet stores) and ask them what their return policy is?
A That's a good idea. I'm glad I _____ (you) today.

11 ▶ Read the article and decide which of the statements below gives the better description of Robin Williams's career.

1. Robin Williams became famous for his roles on television and in movies.
2. Robin Williams's fame can best be attributed to his acting studies and his stand-up comedy routines.

Robin Williams
by Sylvia P. Bloch

"My childhood was kind of lonely and quiet. My father was away working, my mother was away working, and I was basically raised by the maid. I'd spend most of my time alone in our huge house, playing with my toy soldiers." This is how actor-comedian Robin Williams describes his childhood. Born in 1952 in Chicago, Illinois, Williams grew up in Chicago and Detroit and attended eight different schools in eight years because his father, an automobile executive, was frequently transferred.

When his father retired, the family moved to a town near San Francisco, California. Williams went to college and studied political science, but when he discovered theater, he dropped out to pursue acting. After studying in New York City for two years, he returned to San Francisco and started working on his stand-up comedy routines.

Williams began to get noticed and soon received offers to appear on television. His career took off in 1978 with the TV series "Mork & Mindy," where he played the part of Mork, an alien from another planet. Almost 60 million people would tune in to each episode just to watch Williams ad lib and clown around. The show became a hit, and unable to handle the pressure of instant fame, Williams turned to alcohol and drugs.

In 1983, two things happened that influenced Williams to change his life for the better—his friend John Belushi, a fellow comic and actor, died of a drug overdose, and his wife became pregnant. Williams told a magazine, "I knew I couldn't be a father and live that kind of life." He was able to turn his life around.

Williams went on to star in movies, receiving an Academy Award nomination for his role in the film *Good Morning, Vietnam*. He played the part of a grown-up Peter Pan in *Hook* and the part of a divorced father who disguises himself as an English housekeeper in order to be with his children in *Mrs. Doubtfire*.

When the opportunity came to do the voice of the Genie in the Disney movie *Aladdin*, Williams jumped at the chance. He said he wanted to act in something that his children would enjoy, and was very happy when the movie came out and people told him, "I loved it as much as my kid did."

For Robin Williams, being a father is very important. "My kids are the most sobering, most wonderful things in my life."

---

12 ▶ Rewrite the play review, filling in the first blank in each pair with an item from column A and the second blank with an item from column B. Make sure to use the correct tense of the verbs in column A. There is more than one answer for most blanks.

Column A	Column B
call	act (v)
can't imagine	a mistake
consider	a natural comic
find	applauding
make	do
see	extremely funny
watch	laugh
	play
	playing
	the lead character

Compare:
I'm going to *act in* a play.
I'm going to *play the part of* Hamlet.

Surprise of the Theater Season
by Rosanna Stewart

Everyone *watched* child actor Eddie Perez *act* in situation comedies. Audiences _____ him _____ , and critics _____ him _____ .

And so it was a surprise to this critic when the Director of the National Shakespeare Festival Theater _____ Perez _____ in *Hamlet*. I _____ this decision _____ . I _____ this actor _____ a serious part.

However, I went to the opening night, and I _____ Perez _____ the part. And I _____ myself _____ with the rest of the audience. The actor who used to _____ us all _____ has another side to his talent.

13 ▶ Read these short interviews with performers. Rewrite the responses in brackets [ ], combining the two statements and using *before*, *after*, *when*, or *while*. Some items have more than one answer.

1. **A** How did you get interested in singing as a career?
   B [I was going to high school. I sang in the school chorus then.] I guess I decided to be a singer at that time.
   A *How did you get interested in singing as a career?*
   B *While going to high school, I sang in the school chorus. I guess I decided to be a singer at that time.*

2. **A** Did you always know you wanted to be an actor?
   B [I didn't take up drama right away. First, I studied accounting.] I'm glad I changed because I enjoy being an actor.

3. **A** When did you decide to become a theater make-up artist?
   B [I was working as a hairdresser. I got interested in make-up at that time.] I really enjoy doing theater make-up.

4. **A** How did you become a composer?
   B [First, I took guitar lessons. Then I started writing songs for fun.] I became a composer more or less by accident.

5. **A** When did you first realize you wanted to be a dancer?
   B [I went to visit my cousin during summer vacation. I saw my first ballet then.] From that time on, the only thing I ever wanted to do was dance.

14 ▶ Read about the problems of these teenagers. Then say what they hope and wish about the past.

1. Susan tried our for the school chorus, but she doesn't know if she was chosen. She's worried because she didn't practice her song before the tryouts.
   Susan hopes _____ .
   She wishes _____ .

2. Maria's high school offers only one drama class but two music classes. Maria wanted to take drama, but there wasn't enough room in the class. She took music, even though she's more interested in acting, and now she's afraid she failed the test yesterday.
   Maria hopes _____ .
   She wishes _____ .

3. The Drama Club had auditions for a play yesterday. Peter was nervous when he tried out for the part.
   Peter hopes _____ .
   He wishes _____ .

4. Jason likes Polly, another thirteen-year-old in the school band. He's too shy to talk to her, so he wrote her a love letter and put it in her saxophone case. Polly never said anything about the letter.
   Jason hopes _____ .
   He wishes _____ .

15 ► Before you read the article, look carefully at the subtitle. When you have finished reading, say what the two things are that you can't leave to chance.

How to Step Up Your Luck
Two Moves You Can't Leave to Chance

by Catherine Lilly, Ph.D. and Daniel Martin, Ph.D.

What does it mean to be lucky? It commonly means someone who gets something valuable without really trying, someone who is in the right place at the right time. The person who discovers a lost painting by a famous painter, or who buys a winning lottery ticket—these are lucky people. They meet up with unexpectedly fortunate events. Since we have no control over the "when" and the "where" of such events, we can't make them happen to us. The only way to make a difference in our luck is to control ourselves.

Variety can increase your luck

The first rule is to look for variety, new experiences. More variety will result in a richer life with more opportunities. The more varied life is, the more likely that unexpected combinations of events will occur, giving us the chance to improve our situation. Researchers say that being able to change is the best way to survive in changing, unpredictable times. Individuals who can change are more adaptable.

When we are searching for something, like a lost pair of eyeglasses, it isn't a good idea to always follow the same pattern of search. If we always start looking in the basement and systematically work our way through the house, we're probably wasting time. Instead we can learn from the past. Whenever we misplace our glasses, we should start our search at the place where we last found them in order to make use of our past successes. Searching for happiness is like that as well. Be flexible. Learn from your mistakes. Try lots of different possibilities.

Variety is necessary for happiness. No matter how rich our lives may seem, if they consist only of expected events and repetition, boredom steps in.

We find pleasure in the unexpected and the surprising. Birthday presents that we expect do not excite us, but we can be strangely affected by unexpected small signs of generosity or affection. Chance makes the difference. Saying yes to uncertainty adds pleasure to life and contributes to our luck. Sometimes it seems easier, however, to use our strength to build walls to try to protect ourselves from uncertainty. We buy life insurance, household insurance, car insurance. We work hard and put money aside. But all this planning can't guarantee safety. We need to find the courage to welcome uncertainty.

Taking the first step is crucial. Each of us should find one action that will increase variety: subscribe to a new magazine, take a different route to work, sign up for a night-school course. Then focus on its positive results. This positive reinforcement, together with the pleasure of sensing the power in doing what we want to, should give us the courage for the next act.

Saying yes to yourself

Accepting ourselves exactly as we are at this present moment provides the courage to move forward. Believing that all our choices i n the past were the best we could have made at the time frees us from regret and reinforces our belief that we are as good as we can be at this moment. The best preparation for the future is self-acceptance in the present. Self-acceptance and trust in people are the foundations of confidence and courage.

Self-acceptance, courage, and action don't guarantee good luck, but they do guarantee a richer and fuller life. They lead to more opportunities from unexpected events that can enrich our lives.

16 ► As you read the article, pay attention to the authors' suggestions on how to increase your luck. When you have finished reading, say *Right* or *Wrong* for each item below.

The article suggests that people
1. do the same things every day.
2. add variety to their lives and try out new things.
3. be flexible and learn from mistakes.
4. be cautious of new experiences.
5. try to protect themselves from uncertainty.
6. be willing to change.
7. accept themselves as they are.
8. buy life insurance.

17 ► **Tony's friend Marcel is always complaining. Complete Marcel's responses, using an item from box A and a phrase from box B in each of your answers.**

1. **Tony** Let's check out that sale on radios at Radio World.
   Marcel It seems . . .
   Tony *Let's check out that sale on radios at Radio World.*
   Marcel *It seems whenever I buy anything on sale it breaks the next day.*

2. **Tony** There's a dance tonight. Why don't we each ask a date to go with us?
   Marcel I'm sure . . .

3. **Tony** I'm not familiar with Indian food, so will you order for me?
   Marcel I'm sure . . .

4. **Tony** I don't care which movie we see. You pick one out.
   Marcel I'm sure . . .

5. **Tony** Why don't you go get two seats and I'll get the popcorn?
   Marcel I know . . .

6. **Tony** If you'd just study for your tests, you'd do better on them.
   Marcel It seems . . .

Box A	
whatever	however much
whenever	whichever
whoever	wherever

Box B
will say no
will be one you don't want to see
it breaks the next day
you'll think is too spicy
will be too close or too far from the screen for you
I always fail

18 ► **Angela Solera ran into some bad luck. Complete her account of the incident with the correct form of an appropriate three-word verb from the box.**

The other day I _____ file folders, so I went to look for some in Mr. Clemente's desk drawer. Just as I opened the drawer, he _____ and thought I _____ no good. He said I should _____ his files. He thought I was trying to _____ the new job at the company and that I wanted to know who else he was considering for it.

I tried to _____ myself, but he wouldn't listen. He told me to leave his office before he _____ patience. He said he wasn't going to let me _____ such dishonest behavior. I used to _____ Mr. Clemente and I thought he liked me, too. However, I wasn't able to convince him I was innocent, so I guess someone else _____ the new job.

be up to
end up with
find out about
get away with
keep out of
look up to
run out of
stand up for
walk in on

19 ► **These people feel they are unlucky. Give each of them advice, using the information in the article on luck on page 67 and one of the expressions in the box below.**

1. I've bought a lottery ticket at the same store every Friday for five years, but, although most of my friends have won at least once, I never have.
2. Everybody else finds money in the street, but I've walked the same way to school for three years without finding a penny.
3. At work I'm afraid to ask for a raise because, with my luck, the boss would probably fire me.
4. I've had four accidents in four years and I drive the same way to work every day. I know the road perfectly. I don't know what's wrong.
5. I haven't had a vacation in over two years. Every time I get ready to go away, something happens. The airplanes don't have any seats. I lose my passport. I forget to buy travelers checks. There's always something.

It's essential that . . .
It's important that . . .
I recommend that . . .
I suggest that . . .

FUNCTIONS/THEMES	LANGUAGE	FORMS
Identify someone Describe something	Who's the woman (who's) drinking coffee? That's Olga Sandoval. Do you know what *budín de tortilla* is? It's a casserole made with tortillas, chicken, and cheese. I've never seen *Citizen Kane*. What's it about? It's a story modeled on the life of the famous newspaper publisher, William Randolph Hearst.	Relative clauses with pronouns as subjects: Reduced restrictive clauses
Recall something	My teacher used to sit at her desk the whole day, waiting for us to do something wrong.	Placement of adverbs
Describe an activity	He sat in his room all morning playing the guitar. She banged on the wall loudly, making a lot of noise.	

Preview the reading.

1. Do you know what a music video is? Would you rather just listen to music or "see" it as well? Why? Discuss your answers with a partner.

2. Before you read the article on pages 70–71, look at the title and the pictures. What do you think the article is about? Discuss your ideas with a partner.

31. Playing with Music

Ever since music videos became popular in the early 1980s, television viewers have become used to the idea of experiencing music by "seeing" it as well as listening to it. The creation of colorful, artistic music videos allowed millions of viewers to watch visual interpretations of their favorite rock group's songs. Now, thanks to a new technology called CD-ROM (Compact Disc-Read Only Memory), music fans can do more than sit back and listen to music; they can participate in it as well. Imagine directing a music video, recreating your favorite performer's appearance, or composing your own songs—all while sitting at a computer! This new way of experiencing music—called "interactive rock"—is quickly becoming a popular new way for people to enjoy music.

CD-ROM technology allows what was once only possible in your imagination to take place in the comfort of your home. You can listen to, watch, record, and create music, all at the same time.

CD-ROMs look like CDs (compact discs), but unlike ordinary CDs, they store graphics and text in addition to sound. One CD-ROM can store the contents of an entire encyclopedia. A CD-ROM player connects to a computer and supplies it with data. The increased storage capacity of a CD-ROM puts many more choices at the user's disposal than most computer software.

For example, rocker Todd Rundgren's *No World Order*, the first interactive music CD-ROM, allows you to "play" with Rundgren's music. Have you ever thought that a song was too fast or too slow? Interactive rock allows you to make changes. On Rundgren's CD-ROM,

Figure it out

1. **Read the article. If necessary, change your answer to item 2 on page 69.**

2. **A key word in the article is *interactive*. Check (√) the statements that relate to interactive behavior.**

____ 1. Music fans participate in the music.
____ 2. We just sit back and enjoy the song.
____ 3. You can manipulate the graphics on the CD-ROM.
____ 4. The listener can "talk back" to the music.
____ 5. The discs store graphics and text.
____ 6. With the original music videos, you could only listen and watch.
____ 7. You can control the colors and some of the sounds.
____ 8. They never become involved with the music.
____ 9. The audience becomes the performers.

you can select a new tempo with the push of a button. At the same time, you can decide to write new lyrics for his songs, or hear the songs in a different order. Rundgren calls this "your opportunity to talk back to the music."

Using the CD-ROM *Xplora I: Peter Gabriel's Secret World* is a lot like exploring a foreign country. You can choose where you would like to "travel" and what you would like to do. You can manipulate graphics in order to put together parts of rock star Peter Gabriel's face on your computer screen. Or, if you prefer, you can experience the thrill of going backstage with Gabriel at the music industry's annual Grammy award show by viewing realistic graphics and sound. With *Jump: David Bowie Interactive*, you create your own videos of Bowie's songs, and if you press "rewind," you see your video played as many times as you like.

Unlike the experience of listening to music, using interactive CD-ROMs let you control the music. Interactive rock has become so popular that multimedia expert Marc Canter has established the Media Band, the first "software rock and roll band." The Media Band is a collection of images, sounds, and text that the user controls. For example, guitar performances, vocals, and visual effects can all be created by the user. The group exists entirely within the world of "interactive rock" and individual users become the band's managers, producers, and technicians. Media Band lets the audience become the performers.

What is the future of CD-ROM and interactive rock? Singer Lou Reed says that "at a certain point, we'll all

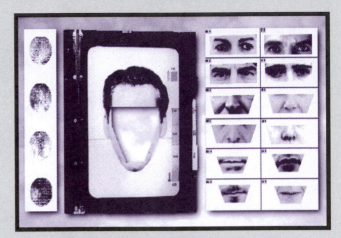

Using the CD-ROM *Xplora I: Peter Gabriel's Secret World*, music fans can construct Gabriel's face on the computer screen.

be dealing with our albums on CD-ROM." Industry analysts agree that people will become increasingly interested in "playing" with music. As interactive rock gains popularity, it is likely that more artists will create exciting CD-ROMs, allowing fans to become more involved in the music than ever.

For now, interactive CD-ROMs offer a choice. As Peter Gabriel explains, "There will be times when you just want to listen to music as a one-sense operation, and there will be other times when you want to sit down and get your hands dirty and play with it."

---

3. **Read the following questions. Then scan the article for the answers.**

1. What are four ways of experiencing music through "interactive rock"?
2. What is a good definition of a CD-ROM?
3. Who is Todd Rundgren and what has he contributed to interactive rock?
4. How can you use the CD-ROM *Xplora I: Peter Gabriel's Secret World*?
5. What does the article say about the future of CD-ROM and interactive rock?

4. **Many words in English stress the first syllable if they are nouns and the second if they are verbs, as in** *record* **[rékərd], a noun, and** *record* **[rikɔ́rd], a verb. Say whether the words in italics are nouns or verbs, and place a stress mark (´) over the correct syllable.**

1. *Record* companies now *produce* CDs.
2. Experts *suspect* that CD-ROM will greatly change the music industry.
3. I'm going to *record* my own version of that song on my computer.
4. My sister is a rock singer. My parents say she's the *rebel* in our family.

32. Do you call *that* singing?

1. Tell your partner who one of your favorite movie stars, singers, or singing groups is. Then describe one of the films or recordings that this person or group has made.

 Paul Cooper is watching music videos on TV when his grandmother comes in.

Listen to the conversation.

2

Mrs. Cooper	Are you watching TV again, Paul? Isn't that the same show that was on yesterday?
Paul	It's not just one show, Grandma. It's actually a lot of different shows. They're music videos.
Mrs. Cooper	Oh, really.
Paul	Why don't you sit down and watch a couple? They're really good.
Mrs. Cooper	Well, I guess it won't hurt. . . . What's that woman with the tambourine supposed to be doing?
Paul	She's singing.
Mrs. Cooper	Do you call *that* singing?
Paul	Sure.
Mrs. Cooper	Hmmm. Music was very different when I was young. It was . . . pleasant. It made you feel happy. It wasn't just a lot of angry noise.
Paul	Music today isn't just angry noise, Grandma. Times are different now.

Mrs. Cooper	I suppose so. . . . What's this, another video?
Paul	Yeah. This one's really cool.
Mrs. Cooper	Who's that guy?
Paul	Which guy?
Mrs. Cooper	The one wearing the crazy hat.
Paul	He's the leader of the band. In the video he plays a normal kid who stands on the corner all day, playing the guitar. Then this big, shiny car comes along . . .
Mrs. Cooper	Oh, let me guess! This "normal kid" stands on a street corner all day waiting for a big, shiny car to come along so he can get his big chance to be a star?
Paul	How did you know?
Mrs. Cooper	I saw it in the movies about 40 years ago. If you don't mind, I think I'll put on my headphones and listen to Julio Iglesias singing *real* music. . . .

3. Combine these sentences. Then shorten them as in the second example sentence.

1. The boy is Paul. The boy is watching music videos.
   The boy who is watching music videos is Paul.
   The boy watching music videos is Paul.

2. The woman is his grandmother. The woman is talking to Paul.

3. The video was on yesterday. The video is on TV now.

4. That guy is the leader of the band. That guy is wearing a crazy hat.

5. The music was quite different. The music was played when Paul's grandmother was young.

72 Unit 7

33. Who's the woman drinking coffee?

1 ▶ Listen to the conversation.
▶ Act out similar conversations. Tell your partner who each person in the illustration is, using the information in the box.

A Who's the woman (who's) drinking coffee?
B That's Olga Sandoval. She's a dancer and she teaches ballet. She's writing a book about dance in Argentina.

The people in the illustration

1. Olga Sandoval is a dancer. She also teaches ballet. She's writing a book about dance in Argentina.
2. Julio Mata is a singer. He has a very good voice and sometimes does opera.
3. Dolores Calderon is a musician. She's very talented and also composes music.

2 ▶ Listen to the two possible conversations.
▶ Act out similar conversations with a partner, using the descriptions in the box.

A Do you know what *budín de tortilla* is?

B Yes. It's a casserole made with tortillas, chicken, and cheese. It's served with chili sauce.

A That sounds delicious. I like anything made with cheese. | **A** I don't really care for things made with cheese.

> *I don't care for* is more polite than *I don't like* when commenting on another person's preferences.

Some foods	Some descriptions
budín de tortilla (Mexico) tempura (Japan) feijoada (Brazil) keftedakia (Greece)	*Budín de tortilla* is a casserole (that is) made with layers of tortillas, chicken, and cheese. It's served with chili sauce. *Tempura* consists of fish, shrimp, and vegetables (that are) dipped in a light batter and fried in oil. *Feijoada* is a stew (that is) made with black beans, beef, pork, and sausage. *Keftedakia* is meatballs (that are) seasoned with mint.

3 ▸ Study the frames: Relative clauses with pronouns as subjects: Reduced restrictive clauses

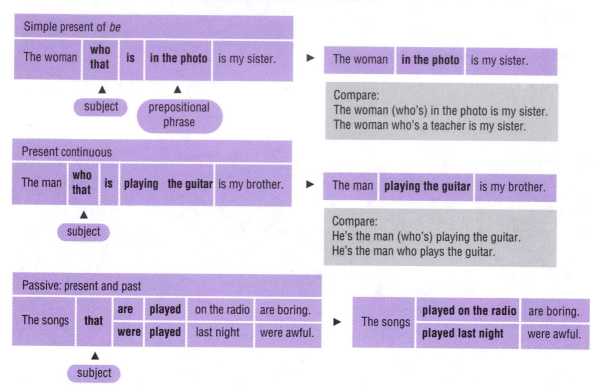

Simple present of *be*

| The woman | who / that | is | in the photo | is my sister. |

▲ subject   ▲ prepositional phrase

▸ The woman **in the photo** is my sister.

Compare:
The woman (who's) in the photo is my sister.
The woman who's a teacher is my sister.

Present continuous

| The man | who / that | is | playing | the guitar | is my brother. |

▲ subject

▸ The man **playing the guitar** is my brother.

Compare:
He's the man (who's) playing the guitar.
He's the man who plays the guitar.

Passive: present and past

| The songs | that | are | played | on the radio | are boring. |
| | | were | played | last night | were awful. |

▲ subject

▸ The songs **played on the radio** are boring.
The songs **played last night** were awful.

4 ▸ Rewrite the description of each movie in the box, reducing the relative clauses.

▸ Act out similar conversations with a partner.

A *I've never seen* Citizen Kane. *What's it about?*

B *It's a story modeled on the life of the famous newspaper publisher, William Randolph Hearst.*

Some classic films

Citizen Kane is a story that is modeled on the life of the famous U.S. newspaper publisher, William Randolph Hearst.

Rashomon is a Japanese movie about a crime that is committed in eleventh-century Japan. It's a story that is told from four different points of view.

Das Boot is a German film about some sailors who are trapped in a submarine. The men that are in the submarine eventually get out alive, but the fate that is awaiting them is just as bad.

La Dolce Vita is a famous Italian film about a journalist who is enjoying the "sweet life" of Rome's high society. At the same time, the journalist is a man who is deeply disturbed by the "sweet life."

RECALL SOMETHING

 5 ▸ Listen to the speakers recall people or experiences they think of when they hear one of the words in the box. For each speaker, write the appropriate word.

1. _____
2. _____
3. _____
4. _____
5. _____

obnoxious	sad
mean	kind
funny	lonely
strict	

6 ▶ **Study the frame: Placement of adverbs**

Adverbs of place, manner, and time

	Place	Manner	Time
He sat	**at his desk**	**quietly**	**all day**.

	Manner	Place	Time
He sat	**quietly**	**at his desk**	**all day**.

Sentences with participial phrases

Adverbs modifying the main verb

	Adverbs	Participial phrases
He sat	**in his room all morning**,	playing the guitar.
She banged	**on the wall loudly**,	making a lot of noise.

Adverbs modifying the verb in the participial phrase

	Participial phrases	Adverbs
She caught the thief,	shooting him	**in the leg**.
He stood there,	listening	**quietly for ten minutes**.

An adverb of manner ending in *-ly* may also precede the participial phrase.
He stood there, *quietly* listening.

Sentences with two meanings

The position of the comma (,) shows which verb an adverb modifies.
   He stood there, quietly listening to his friends. (He listened quietly.)
   He stood there quietly, listening to his friends. (He stood quietly.)

The use of a comma shows which noun is the subject of the verb in the participial phrase.
   She caught the thief, shooting him in the leg. (She shot the thief.)
   She caught the thief shooting him in the leg. (The thief shot somebody.)

7 ▶ **Restate the conversations, combining the sentences in brackets [ ] into one sentence and putting the adverbs followed by a slash (/) in their correct positions. Check to make sure you have used commas correctly, when they are needed.**

1. **A** Wasn't yesterday a beautiful day?
   B It sure was. [for hours/outside/I just sat. I was reading a book.]
   A *Wasn't yesterday a beautiful day?*
   B *It sure was. I just sat outside for hours, reading a book.*

2. **A** Did you hear John was fired last week?
   B Yes, Sally told me. [They caught him. secretly/He was looking through his boss's files.]

3. **A** I don't know what I'm going to do with my son. [all day/in his room/He sits. He listens to loud music.]
   B Mine isn't any better. [on a street corner/He spends hours. He talks to his friends.]

4. **A** I think there's something wrong with my neighbor.
   B Why do you say that?
   A [Last night I was at home. quietly/I was playing the piano.] It wasn't even 8:30 and he started knocking on my wall.

34. Your turn

1. Work with your classmates. Talk about each of the different types of music pictured here. What do you know about each one? Which singers and musicians do you know who perform the different types of music?

2. Choose one type of music that you like best. Work with a partner who also likes this kind of music and share your impressions. What are some of your favorite songs? Who are your favorite performers? Have you ever seen this music performed live? What do you like most about this type of music? Can you remember the words to any songs? Can you sing a song? Report your ideas to the class.

country western

classical

rock 'n' roll

salsa

rap

jazz

reggae

☰ Listen in

A musician is being interviewed on WKHZ radio. Listen to the interview and then say what type of music the musician performs.

35. On your own

1. Imagine that you went to one of the performances in the photos. Write a review for a local magazine or newspaper.

opera

Broadway musical

Kabuki theater

ballet

mime

Ballet Fólklorico

2. Write a short biography of a performer whose music you enjoy. Include important facts about his or her life and interesting information about his or her music. Tell what makes this performer so popular.

PREVIEW

FUNCTIONS/THEMES	LANGUAGE	FORMS
Convince someone	There's a computer technology conference that I would like to attend. It's a very important meeting and I think it's essential that I go. It's very important for me to keep up to date on what's going on.	Subjunctive clauses vs. infinitive clauses
Inform someone	It is essential for us to fill the vacancy left by Mr. Franco.	
Make judgments	Karen just bought a new television and a stereo and now she wants a personal computer. You know what they say: The more you get, the more you want.	Double comparatives
Give advice	Speed limits have a purpose, and the sooner you start paying attention to them, the better for everyone.	
Ask someone to do something	Oh, Larry, could you help me for a minute, please? Excuse me, Dr. Bellini. I wonder if you could help me for just a minute, please. Melissa, I'd like you to help me for a minute, please.	

Preview the reading.

Student A
You are the office manager at a large accounting firm. Student B is your employee and has just arrived at the office, late for the third time this week. Student B does excellent work, but the chronic lateness has become a topic of discussion among the other employees. Talk to this employee and try to resolve the problem.

Student B
You are an employee at a large accounting firm. You just haven't felt like going to work the past few days so you've been arriving fifteen or twenty minutes late. Although you like your work, you feel a need to be more independent and creative at your job.

36. How Do Real Managers

You're irresponsible and lazy. Be here at 9:00 A.M. from now on!

Wrong

by
*Kermit
Moore*

An employee comes to you with a suggestion about changing the budgeting process. You think it's wildly impractical. Do you tell the employee that the budget really isn't his or her area and that someone else will take care of it? Not if you want an involved, motivated employee. When you take a negative approach toward your workers, you merely send them the underlying message that they are stupid not to know their places and even stupider not to stay in them. The result: defensive and alienated employees. Yet too many managers simply aren't sensitive to the message behind their words. Here are some reminders about how to communicate to get results:

● **Realize that communication involves risks.** "Every time you open your mouth, you are taking a risk," says Dr. Gay Lumsden, a professor at Kean College in Union, New Jersey, and a management consultant. "You are risking rejection—of yourself, your ideas, your values, your opinions. And when your employees talk to you, they are not only taking these risks, they are risking their jobs and their careers as well."

Most of us take rejection of our ideas personally, so effective managers are careful to show appreciation and sensitivity, says Lumsden. Managers should never feel that they must agree with an employee, of course, but by acknowledging a worker's idea before they dismiss it, they create an atmosphere that invites participation, cooperation, innovation, and creativity.

● **When criticizing someone, describe, don't judge.** "Always focus on, and confine criticism to, observable behavior," advises Dr. Linda Eagle, a manager at Arthur Andersen and Company's Management Information Consulting Division. For instance, telling someone who's consistently late, "You've been coming in late, and we need

you here on time," is more likely to encourage promptness than snapping, "You're irresponsible and lazy. Be here at 9:00 A.M. from now on." The time for determining that a person is irresponsible is in a formal performance evaluation, says Eagle.

● **Focus on goals rather than image.** Take the example of a manager who drops a report on the desk of an assistant and says, "Photocopy this for me." If photocopying is the secretary's responsibility, not the assistant's, the manager is obviously going out of his or her way to remind the assistant who's boss. The manager may get the copy, but he or she may also get a defensive assistant along with it. What's more, since defensiveness often leads to more defensiveness, the manager and the assistant will now be locked in a bitter power struggle, with both trying to protect their self-esteem and defend their positions. Therefore, the manager would do better to request, rather than demand, a copy from an assistant.

● **Remember to show recognition, acknowledgment, and appreciation.** Surveys suggest that workers want, above all, to be acknowledged for a job well done, says Dr. Barry Eisenberg, director of employee education at the Memorial Sloan-Kettering Cancer Research Center in New York. Lumsden adds that "one of the best ways to acknowledge workers is to bring them into the day-to-day processes of the business: Listen to their ideas, share information, encourage creativity, let them know you value their input."

Above all, be consistent with praise and punishment. People feel more self-confident and more willing to take chances about being innovative when they know what to expect from their bosses.

Communicate?

You've been coming in late, and we need you here on time.

Right

Figure it out

1. **As you read the article, pay careful attention to the suggestions given for effective communication between managers and employees. When you have finished, say *Effective* or *Ineffective* for each of the manager's comments below. For each comment, identify a statement in the article that supports your answer.**

   1. You don't have time to think of ideas for the new project. Your job is to finish the old one.
   2. It's very important that you be on time for your appointments. I've noticed that you've kept a few clients waiting more than 15 minutes.
   3. This letter is excellent, and I can see you've put a lot of thought into it. There are only a few small changes I'd like you to make.
   4. Your coworkers tell me you're uncooperative. I suggest you change your attitude.
   5. I know this isn't part of your job, but I'd really appreciate it if you could file these papers.

2. **Imagine that you write a weekly advice column on business. A frustrated manager writes to you complaining that an employee has been taking long weekends by calling in sick every Monday. Based on what you have learned from the article, write a short letter to "Frustrated," giving advice on what to say to the employee.**

3. **The prefix *self-* may be placed before many words, as in *self-esteem* and *self-confident*. Complete each sentence with one of the words below, using your dictionary if necessary.**

   self-confidence   self-destructive
   self-control   self-sufficient

   1. Tony is very _____ for a ten-year-old. He even cooks his own meals.
   2. Lola does excellent work, but she lacks _____ . She finds something wrong with everything she does.
   3. Louis stays out late every night, comes to work late every morning, and even insults his boss. I think he's really _____ .
   4. Nancy has no _____ . She's always losing her temper over nothing.

37. Maybe you'd better stay here after all!

1. You want to do one of the following things with your partner who isn't interested. Try to persuade your partner to change his or her mind.

1. Skip class tomorrow and go to a movie.
2. Take a weekend bike trip.
3. Invite the class to one of your houses for a party.
4. Sign up for a self-defense class like karate.

 Linda Rueda and her boss, Sam Greene, work for an architectural firm. They are in Guadalajara on business.

Listen to the conversation.

2

Sam Listen, Linda . . . I'm afraid you're going to have to cut your trip short. Bill had to go into the hospital suddenly, so there's no one back home supervising things.

Linda The hospital! What happened to him?

Sam Well, it seems he had an appendicitis attack. The doctor told him it was essential that he be operated on right away.

Linda Oh, well, I suppose we should be glad it wasn't anything more serious. Is it really necessary for me to go home, though? I would think everyone could manage without us for a week.

Sam Well, I'm worried about the new project. I can't emphasize enough how important it is for us to get that contract.

Linda Do you mean the shopping center? I'm sure Ray and Nancy can handle it. You know they're very capable, Sam, and the more responsibility we give them, the less work we'll have in the long run.

Sam In principle, I agree with you. But in this particular case I'd feel more comfortable if you were there. I think the sooner you get back, the better.

Linda Well, I'll change my plans then. Still, there's one point I think I should mention. The people we're scheduled to meet with here on Monday don't speak any English.

Sam Oh! Well, uh . . . hmm . . . it looks as if maybe you'd better stay here after all!

3. Check (√) the statements that are stated or implied in the conversation.

_____ 1. Linda wasn't planning to leave Guadalajara so soon.
_____ 2. Bill got appendicitis in Guadalajara.
_____ 3. Linda thinks there are more serious illnesses than appendicitis.
_____ 4. Bill needed to have surgery immediately.
_____ 5. Bill was handling the shopping center contract when he became ill.

_____ 6. Linda wants to go back home right away.
_____ 7. Sam thinks Ray and Nancy can handle the shopping center contract by themselves.
_____ 8. Linda thinks Ray and Nancy should be given more responsibility.
_____ 9. Sam speaks Spanish.
_____ 10. Linda speaks Spanish.

38. It's very important that I keep up to date...

1 ► Listen to the conversation.
   ► Act out similar conversations. You would like to attend a conference, take a course, or give a speech at a meeting. Using your notes, try to convince your boss that the activity is important.

A Excuse me, Mr. Harwood. Could I speak to you for a minute?

B Yes, of course, Sylvia. What is it?

A I'll get right to the point. There's a computer technology conference that I would like to attend in Houston next month.

B Oh?

A Yes. It's a very important meeting and I think

it's essential | that I / for me to | go.

B I'm not sure it's really necessary. And, anyway, I'm not sure the company can afford it.

A Well, sir, it happens to be my field, and I think

it's very important | that I / for me to | keep up to date

on what's going on—for the company's sake.

B Well, maybe you have a point. I'll give it some thought.

Computer Technology Conference
• Houston, next month
• important meeting
• essential to go
• it happens to be in my field
• important to keep up to date for company's sake

Course in English Conversation
• begins in two weeks
• interesting course
• important to enroll
• I happen to know some English
• crucial to learn English for international meetings

MEETING OF THE NATIONAL ORGANIZATION
• I'VE BEEN INVITED TO SPEAK ON FRIDAY
• THE LARGEST ORGANIZATION OF
• IMPORTANT TO ATTEND
• THERE WILL BE MANY WELL-KNOWN PEOPLE THERE
• IMPORTANT TO REPRESENT THE COMPANY

2 ► Study the frames: Subjunctive clauses vs. infinitive clauses

Subjunctive clauses

| It's | important necessary essential urgent crucial | that | I you he she we they | learn | Spanish. |
| | | | | be | there. |

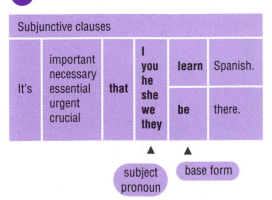
subject pronoun · base form

Infinitive clauses

| It's | important necessary essential urgent crucial | for | me you him her us them | to learn | Spanish. |
| | | | | to be | there. |

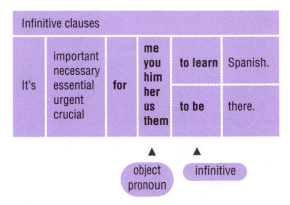
object pronoun · infinitive

3 ▶ **Rewrite this memo about the warehouse of a publishing company. Change the subjunctive clauses to infinitive clauses and the infinitive clauses to subjunctive clauses.**

Start like this:
It is essential for us to fill the vacancy. . . .

INTEROFFICE MEMORANDUM

TO: Clifford Olsen, Personnel
FROM: Paula Davis
SUBJECT: Vacancy left by Mr. Franco

It is essential that we fill the vacancy left by Mr. Franco. Because of our current workload, it is urgent for us to do this immediately. As for qualifications, it is crucial that the candidate have previous warehouse experience, and since we have many Spanish-speaking customers, it is also important that he or she have a knowledge of that language.

I am confident that I can leave the matter of finding a replacement in your hands. Please bear in mind that it is crucial for the warehouse to have a full staff. The sooner this is accomplished, the better.

Thank you for your help in this matter.

 4 ▶ **Listen and match each conversation with the picture it describes.**

5 ▶ **Study the frame: Double comparatives**

The	**more work**	we give her,	the	**less work**	we'll have.		of nouns
	angrier	she became,		**more depressed**	I got.		of adjectives
	louder	he yelled,		**more quietly**	I spoke.	◀	of adverbs
	more	she talked,		**less**	I listened.		of verbs

One kind of comparative may appear in a sentence with any other kind. The *faster* he drove, the *more nervous* I got. (comparative of adverb and comparative of adjective)

6

▶ **Listen to the conversation.**

▶ **Act out similar conversations. You are a police officer who has stopped your partner for one of the offenses in the box. Tell him or her to be more cautious.**

A I'm sorry, Officer. I wasn't paying attention.

B Listen, I'm going to give you some advice. Slow down! When you're speeding, you're taking your life, and very possibly someone else's, in your hands.

A Yes, I realize that. I'm sorry. I just wasn't thinking.

B Well, you'd better start thinking. You have to remember that you aren't the only one on the road. Speed limits have a purpose, and the sooner you start paying attention to them, the better for everybody!

A Yes. You're right. Thanks for the advice.

Some offenses
speeding (not paying attention to speed limits) crossing the street against the light (ignoring traffic lights) turning without signaling (not using turn signals)

7 ▶ **Work with a partner. Student A: Tell your partner about a problem you have and ask for advice.**
Student B: Give advice to Student A, using double comparatives.

A *I can't find an apartment that I can afford.*

B *I think you should keep looking. The more you look, the better chance you have of finding something.*

8 ▶ **The way you ask someone to do something for you depends on who you are speaking to. First, practice the conversations below. Then play the role of one of the people in the box and ask for help or ask a favor appropriately.**

To an equal: a doctor to another doctor

A Oh, Larry, *could you help me for a minute, please?* I can't seem to find the file on Joyce Rollins.

B Sure, Rita.

To a boss: a nurse to a doctor

A Excuse me, Dr. Bellini. *I wonder if you could help me for just a minute, please.* I can't seem to find the vaccine you said was in the refrigerator.

B Sure, Amanda.

To an employee: a doctor to a receptionist

A Melissa, *I'd like you to help me for a minute, please.* I lost the list of this afternoon's patients that you gave me.

B Certainly, Dr. Engel.

Some situations at a doctor's office
Amanda Vega, a nurse, has dropped a contact lens and asks Larry Bellini, a doctor, to help her find it. Rita Engel, a doctor, usually locks up the office at night. Today she has to leave early because of an emergency at the hospital, so she asks Dr. Bellini to lock up. Dr. Engel asks Melissa Dale, a receptionist, to call two patients, Mrs. Chen and Mr. Adamski, to reschedule their appointments.

39. Your turn

1. **Work with a group. You are a member of a planning team whose goal it is to decide where to hold a big international conference of travel agents next year. Look at the photos and read the descriptions to decide which city should host the conference. Talk about each city and discuss the advantages and disadvantages of holding the conference there.**

Kyoto, Japan Founded in 794, in the beautiful setting of a river valley surrounded by mountains, Kyoto was Japan's capital until 1600. It remains the center of traditional Japanese culture today. Kyoto has several hundred Buddhist temples and Shinto shrines, many parks and gardens, several architecturally outstanding palaces—each with its own impressive gardens—and over thirty colleges and universities. Kyoto is also a modern city, as important for its large industries as for its silks, ceramics, and other crafts.

Salvador de Bahia, Brazil Salvador de Bahia, the first Portuguese settlement in Brazil, was founded in 1549. Located on All Saints Bay, it is divided into an Upper City, on cliffs overlooking the bay, and a Lower City; the two are connected by elevators as well as by roads. Salvador is known for its colonial architecture— especially its elaborate churches—for its beautiful beaches, and as a center for African culture, brought over to Brazil by slaves long ago. Salvador is also one of Brazil's main ports and a center of industry.

Taxco, Mexico Located in southwestern Mexico, Taxco was founded by Spaniards in 1529 and soon became important for its silver mines. Since modern architecture is prohibited, Taxco preserves much of its colonial character—its steep cobblestone streets are lined with white stucco houses, which have red tile roofs and wrought-iron balconies filled with colorful flowers. In addition to its beauty, Taxco is known for its many silver shops, which produce and sell the finest jewelry and other silverwork in Mexico.

Volendam, the Netherlands Volendam is located in Ijsselmeer, a freshwater lake separated from the North Sea by a dike. It is famous as a fishing village, as well as for the traditional costumes of the women, especially their winged lace caps. Volendam is only 11 miles from Amsterdam, one of Europe's most exciting cities.

2. Work with a partner. Play these roles.

Student A You are the head of the management committee of Worldwide Travel, Inc., a large travel organization with branch offices in many different cities. Because sales have gone down over the last three years, you have decided that it is impossible for you to send travel agents from the different offices to a big international conference of travel agents. Tomorrow you will meet with Student B, the head of a group of managers from different offices. Student B will try to convince you to change your mind. Look at the memo, a page from the conference brochure, and the graph. Then reply to Student B's arguments.

Student B You work for Worldwide Travel, Inc., a large travel organization with branch offices in many different cities. You are the head of a group of managers from the different offices. Student A, the head of the main office, has decided that there is no money in the budget to send travel agents from the branch offices to the conference. Tomorrow you will meet with Student A to discuss this issue. Look at the memo, a page from the conference brochure, and the graph. Then try to convince Student A to change his or her mind.

MEMO

TO: Management Committee
FROM: Joanne Wagner,
        Manager—Southwest Office
DATE: May 14
RE: International Conference

You may be interested in knowing that travel agents in our office feel that it is essential that they attend the international conference in

The Conference will include workshops on:

- promoting off-season tourism
- increasing peak-season travel
- sales personnel effectiveness
- advances in computer technology

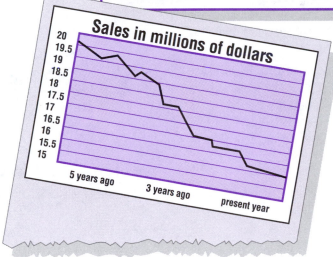

🔊 Listen in

Amy Britt works at Worldwide Travel, Inc. She has conversations with three different people in her office. Read the questions below. Then listen to the conversations and answer the questions.

1. In each conversation, who is Ms. Britt talking to? Choose *a, b,* or *c.*
   a. her boss
   b. a coworker
   c. an employee who works for her

2. Who ends up picking up the brochures?

40. On your own

1. Write a memo to your boss explaining why you think he or she should send you to one of the conferences featured in the posters.

MANAGEMENT SEMINAR & RETREAT

at "The Mountainside Resort"
in Seattle, Washington

Audience: Mid-level management personnel from any size company

° Overview of advances in computer technology
° Dealing with "High Tech Stress"
° The diplomacy of effective management
° Handling employee complaints
° "Letting go" without losing control

For information and reservations, call The Management Consortium 1-800-555-2121

LEARN HOW TO REALLY INTERACT!

Attend the Annual "Information Highway" Conference in Aspen, Colorado

• TV, modems, & networking
• Communicating via electronic bulletin boards
• The latest about virtual reality
• Video conferences

Package includes:
– Excellent hotel accommodations next to the Conference Center
– International gourmet dinner evening
– Optional ski package

For more information, call Internetworks, Inc.
1-800-555-2000

2. **Choose one of the options below.**

1. Write a memo to your employee explaining why you think he or she should attend one of the conferences featured in the posters.
2. Write a memo to your real boss. Try to convince him or her to make a change you think is necessary in your company.

FUNCTIONS/THEMES	LANGUAGE	FORMS
Talk about plans Give reasons	What are your plans for the future? After I graduate, I'll get a job and work for five or ten years. By then, I will have gotten some experience. I've decided to quit my job. You're kidding! I'm surprised to hear that. By the end of this year, I will have been working for the company for four years, and I haven't even had a promotion yet.	The future perfect and the future perfect continuous
Make predictions	Futurist Ronald Herd feels that dwellings will have changed significantly by the year 2025.	
Imagine something Give explanations	What do you suppose your life would be like if you hadn't finished high school? Well, I suppose I'd be working in a boring job somewhere, and I probably wouldn't speak a word of English. Whenever I talk to Chris, he laughs, even when we're talking about something serious. I'm sure if he weren't so nervous, he wouldn't laugh all the time.	Mixed contrary-to-fact conditional sentences: Present and past

Preview the reading.

1. Discuss these questions with a partner.
   a. What is the illustration below about?
   b. Have you ever had your fortune told? If so, what was it?
   c. What kinds of fortunetelling or prediction do people use in your country? Do you believe in any of them? Why or why not?

2. Before you read the article on pages 90–91, look at the title and the photos. What kinds of fortunetelling do you think the article discusses?

41.
The ANCIENT ART OF PREDICTION

by Leanna Skarnulis

After winning the Nobel Prize in 1957, two physicists from the United States, Chen Ning Yang and Tsung-Dao Lee, faced the question of whether or not to continue their research. They consulted the *I Ching,* the ancient Chinese book of prophecy. It assured them that a breakthrough in particle physics would be achieved in the next two years. The two scientists continued their work.

Today, many people who have been influenced by the modern scientific age rarely use fortunetelling for anything other than amusement, but it wasn't always so. Before the arrival of the scientific method, with its demand for proof, most people believed that the future could be foretold, and they had countless ways of doing it.

Fortunetellers had to be inventive because the art of prophecy was a risky business. When a prophecy failed, fortunetellers would deal with their predicament by coming up with an explanation and then proposing a new, improved method. Here are some of the more creative methods that have been used to forecast the future.

Both ordinary and unusual objects may contain prophetic signs. If someone gives you a black pearl, a sapphire, or a weapon, beware of bad luck. On the other hand, you should be glad to get a white rat or white mouse, for they bring good luck.

Onomancy is prophecy from first names. Aurelia will be intelligent and likely to remain single. Armand will let success with women go to his head, miss an opportunity, and finally marry just anyone.

Dominoes laid face down and then turned over have prophetic meaning; but don't consult them on Monday or Friday because bad luck will follow. Each domino in the set has meaning. The double blank is the worst to draw for it indicates great disappointment in love, school, or business; however, for dishonest people, it predicts success in their dishonest activities.

Coffee grounds can be read by pouring grounds and water onto a white plate and draining off the water after the grounds settle. The figures are then interpreted. Several broken lines mean money troubles, an elephant means success, and thick and rounded blots foretell a lawsuit.

Even shoes have been used in prophecy. Young women wanting to know if they will marry can throw a shoe downstairs. If the shoe lands with the toe propped up, no marriage will take place. If the heel end is up, the marriage will occur in as many days, months, or years as the number of steps the shoe falls down.

Other familiar objects, such as paper and playing cards, also figure in prophecy. Tarot cards, a set of twenty-two playing cards, contain special pictures that depict vices and virtues. The hanged-man card, for instance, frequently indicates spiritual growth.

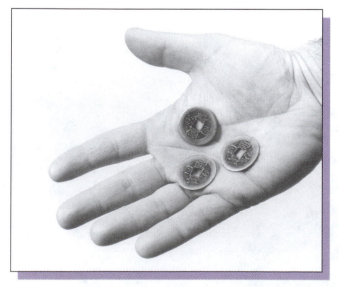

I Ching coins. For their meaning, consult the *I Ching,* a Chinese book of prophecy.

Notice the double blank in this set of dominoes (second row, far left).

Curiously, though, with the exception of some fortunetelling computers in shopping centers and carnivals, few prophetic methods involve modern objects. Perhaps the fortunetellers have not been able to keep up with the pace of change. But one day the results of our technology just might include prophecy by clothes dryer, where people study the arrangement of shorts and towels at the end of a cycle, or prophecy by laser price codes, where people study the order and number of wide and narrow stripes on canned tuna. Perhaps these methods sound far-fetched, but it is probably safe to say that modern disillusionment with science and renewed interest in fortunetelling will lead to innovations.

And what finally happened to the physicists who consulted the *I Ching*? Remember that they were assured that a breakthrough in particle physics would occur very soon. It actually came in 1963 and involved application of their earlier principles, but it was two other physicists—Val L. Fitch and James W. Cronin—who made the breakthrough. They received the 1980 Nobel Prize in physics.

Tarot cards from Spain, in a traditional fortunetelling pattern.

Figure it out

1. Choose *a*, *b*, or *c*.

The main purpose of this article is to
   a. explain why fortunetelling was popular.
   b. describe methods of fortunetelling and comment on its future.
   c. make a judgment on whether fortunetelling is reliable.

2. As you read, try to remember which prophetic signs bring good luck and which bad luck. When you have finished, say *Good luck* or *Bad luck* for each of the items below. Then skim the article again to check your answers, and make any necessary corrections.

1. receiving a white rat or white mouse
2. naming a child Armand
3. the double-blank domino (for honest people)
4. broken lines or rounded blots in the figures formed by coffee grounds
5. a shoe that lands with the toe pointing up when it is thrown down a flight of stairs by a young woman who wants to know if she will marry
6. the hanged-man Tarot card

3. Do you feel that the author personally believes in the prophecies she discusses? What does she say in the article to support your answer?

4. The suffix *-ist* refers to people and has several different meanings. Give the correct words for the following, using your dictionary if necessary.

Someone who specializes in . . .
1. physics   2. chemistry   3. science

Someone who . . .
4. writes novels   5. plays the cello

Someone who believes in . . .
6. capitalism   7. communism   8. socialism

42. You'll have a lucky break.

1. Tell your partner what you think you'll be doing in the future. Mention topics such as where you plan to live, what kind of job you think you'll have, and whether you'll be married and have a family.

June Sanders, a young veterinarian, is visiting a fortuneteller.

Listen to the conversation.

②

Fortuneteller	Let's begin by seeing what's in your cards. *(Shuffles and lays out the cards)* Hmm . . . I see a big change in your life . . . not immediately, perhaps, but five or six years from now. Yes, by then you will have been married for a couple of years.
June	What? Me, married?
Fortuneteller	Yes. To a musician—a musician with green eyes and black hair.
June	Not my friend Anton? You must be kidding! Why, the thought never crossed my mind.
Fortuneteller	Well, it's certainly crossed his.
June	What about the big change in my life? The first thing you mentioned?
Fortuneteller	Ah, yes. You'll have a lucky break in five or six years. Your financial worries will be a thing of the past.
June	That's nice to hear! If I hadn't opened that animal hospital, I'd have a lot more money right now. It's used up all of my savings.
Fortuneteller	*(Flips cards)* In the meantime, you must be very careful, though. Someone has a grudge against you.
June	Oh, no! Against me? Who could it be?
Fortuneteller	It's someone who knows your future husband. Apparently, you've offended him. If he weren't so shy, he would have confronted you already. But he still wants to get even with you.
June	What do you mean "get even with me"?
Fortuneteller	I don't know. But don't get too alarmed. You're not in any physical danger. I'm only telling you about this because by this time next week, you will have received a letter from him.
June	Are you serious?
Fortuneteller	Yes, and it's essential that you answer it *very* carefully.

3. A prediction is a statement someone makes about what he or she thinks will happen in the future. Based on the dialogue, say *Prediction* or *Fact* for each sentence below.

1. In five or six years, June will have been married for a couple of years.
2. June has a friend named Anton who is a musician with green eyes and black hair.
3. June used up all of her savings to open an animal hospital.
4. By this time next week, June will have received a letter from someone who knows her future husband.
5. June is visiting a fortuneteller in order to find out about her future.

43. What are your plans for the future?

1 ▶ **Listen to the conversation.**
▶ **Act out similar conversations. Tell your partner what you would like to do in the future. Use your own ideas or the information in the boxes below.**

A What are your plans for the future?
B My dream is to open my own business someday. After I graduate, I'll get a job and work for five or ten years. By then, I will have gotten some experience and I can go off on my own.
A What kind of business would you like to start?
B I think a clothing store might be nice. I've always been interested in fashion.

I'd like to . . .
open my own business.
get a job as a _____ .
move to _____ .
have children.
spend a year in an English-speaking country.

By then I will have . . .
gotten some experience.
finished school.
lived here for _____ years.
saved more money.
been studying English for _____ years.

2 ▶ **Listen to the conversation.**
▶ **Act out similar conversations. Tell your partner about a decision you have made and explain your reasons for it.**

A I've decided to quit my job.
B You're kidding! I'm surprised to hear that.
A Well, by the end of this year, I will have been working for the company for four years, and I haven't even had a promotion yet. I feel that . . .

You've decided to . . .
quit your job because you've been working for the company for almost four years and haven't had a promotion.
stop studying English because you've been studying it for almost six years and are getting bored.
go back to your country/hometown because you've been away for almost five years and are getting homesick.

3 ▶ **Study the frames: The future perfect and the future perfect continuous**

The future perfect					
By then	he	will	have	mailed	it.
	June	won't		spoken	to him.

The future perfect continuous						
By then	I	will	have	been	working	for years.
	she	won't			teaching	very long.

The future perfect
Use the future perfect to talk about an event in the future that will take place before another event.
By the time you get here, I will have eaten. (I'll eat dinner before you arrive.)
Use the future perfect to talk about a state that will already be in progress when an event takes place.
By the time my wife stops working, I *will have been* retired for two years.

The future perfect continuous
Use the future perfect continuous to talk about an activity that will already be in progress when an event takes place.
By the time you come to Spain, I *will have been living* there for almost a year.
Do not use the future perfect continuous with verbs such as *be*, *have*, *want*, or *like* that describe states.

4 ► Rewrite this book review of *Modern Living*, completing the sentences with the future perfect or the future perfect continuous forms of the verbs in parentheses.

MODERN LIVING *by Ronald Herd*
208 pp New York Bookworld, Inc.
$18.95
by Gabriela Alvarez

Imagine that the year is 2025 and that you are looking for a place to live. What will your house or apartment be like? Futurist Ronald Herd feels that dwellings _____ (change) significantly by then. In his new book, *Modern Living,* Herd says that architects _____ (stop) building single-family homes because of lack of space, and most people _____ (move) into apartment buildings.

According to Mr. Herd, apartments themselves will be much smaller and will not have living rooms. In fact, by then architects _____ (design) apartments without living rooms for some time, so most people _____ (get) used to them. However, Mr. Herd warns us that housing certainly _____ (not become) any less expensive. So start saving your money now!

---

 5 ► Listen to the conversation.
► Act out similar conversations, using your own information or the information in the box below. Imagine that something in your past had been different. Tell your partner what you think your life would be like today.

A Did you finish high school?

B Yes. Fortunately.

A What do you suppose your life would be like if you hadn't finished?

B Well, I suppose I'd be working in a boring job somewhere and I probably wouldn't speak a word of English.

B Oh, things probably wouldn't be much different.

Suppose you had(n't) . . .

finished high school.
gone to college.
been the only child in your family.
left home when you finished school.
lived abroad.

---

6 ► Study the frame: Mixed contrary-to-fact conditional sentences with past condition and present result

Past condition		Present result	
If	**I had (I'd) been** more practical,	**I would (I'd) have** more money now.	► *If I had been more practical* means "I wasn't more practical."
	I hadn't moved here,	**I would (I'd) be living** in Italy now.	► *If I hadn't moved here* means "I did move here."

▲ past perfect form of verb

▲ present conditional

7 ▸ **Study the frame: Mixed contrary-to-fact conditional sentences with present condition and past result**

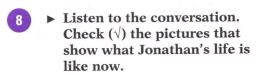

Present condition		Past result
If	he **weren't** so shy,	he **would have called** you.
	she **liked** him,	she **wouldn't have been rude** to him.

past form of verb

past conditional

▸ *If he weren't so shy* means "He is shy."

▸ *If she liked him* means "She doesn't like him."

8 ▸ **Listen to the conversation. Check (√) the pictures that show what Jonathan's life is like now.**

9 ▸ **The director of an archeology expedition to South America has just hired six field assistants to go with him. Complete his conversation with another archeologist. Use the correct forms of the verbs in parentheses.**

A Well, how did you make out?

B I hired six excellent students, but I wish I could have hired more. If they _____ (allow) me to hire more than six students, I _____ (feel) a lot happier right now.

A Why is that?

B I _____ (not disappoint) so many people. There were a lot of other good candidates, and they were all so interested and eager.

A Anyone I know?

B Alex Dua. He knows a lot about archeology, but I thought he'd have a lot of difficulty getting along in a foreign country. He's not very outgoing, unfortunately. If he _____ (not be) such a shy person, I _____ (ask) him to join the expedition. Then there's Nancy Ryder. She's very qualified, but her Spanish is quite poor. If she _____ (speak) better Spanish, I think I definitely _____ (hire) her, too.

10 ▸ **Listen to the conversation.**
▸ **Act out similar conversations with a partner. You are puzzled by the behavior of the people described in the box. Your partner will try to explain why they act as they do.**

A You know Chris better than I do. Maybe you can explain something.

B Maybe. What is it?

A Well, whenever I talk to him, he laughs, even when we're talking about something serious.

B Oh, don't let it bother you. Chris is just a very nervous person. Why don't you talk to him about it? I'm sure if he weren't so nervous, he wouldn't laugh all the time.

Some people who behave strangely
Whenever you talk to Chris he laughs, even when the topic is serious.
Helene keeps borrowing money from you, but she never pays it back. She still owes you twenty dollars from two weeks ago.
You invited Raul and three of your friends to dinner last week. Raul seemed very uncomfortable and hardly said a word the whole evening.
You're always very open with Lillian, but she never seems to want to talk about herself. You can't understand why not.

Some reasons for their behavior
Chris is a very nervous person.
Helene is a very absent-minded person.
Raul is an awfully shy person.
Lillian has had a lot of health problems in the past year.

44. Your turn

Look at the pictures and read the information about Blake Hudson and Sofia Estrada. Working in groups, discuss the choices open to Blake and Sofia that are given in the box below, and try to predict what the consequences of each choice would be. Then, as a group, decide what you think Blake and Sofia should do.

Blake and Sofia's choices

1. Blake and Sofia can forget each other, get married now, or separate and plan to get married at some future date.
2. Blake can return to the United States and take the job there, give up that job and try to get a job in Ecuador, or stay in Ecuador and do something else.
3. Sofia can finish medical school in Ecuador, try to continue her studies in the United States, postpone finishing her studies, or give up medical school completely.

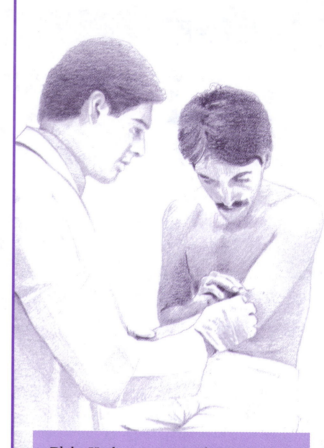

Blake Hudson is a specialist in infectious diseases from the United States. He's in Ecuador on a special one-year research program. He's supposed to leave in March to take an important job at Jackson Memorial Hospital in Miami. Blake is extremely good at his work. He's also very lucky to have been offered the job in Miami.

SOUTH AMERICA

ECUADOR

Esmeraldas
★ QUITO
Manta • • Ambato
Guayaquil
• Cuenca
Salinas

Isla Isabela • Isla San Salvador
Isla Fernandina • Isla Santa Cruz
Isla San Cristobal

Galápagos Islands

Sofia Estrada is a medical student from Ecuador. She still has one more year of medical school to complete and then a year of residency. Sofia has had to work her way through medical school, and she has made a lot of sacrifices to do so.

Blake and Sofia met at the hospital where she's studying, and they fell in love. They've talked about getting married, and the time has come to make some choices.

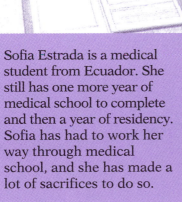 ## Listen in

Read the question below. Then listen to the conversation between Blake and Sofia and answer the question.

What are both Blake and Sofia afraid of?

Would you have a similar fear if you were Blake or Sofia? Do you think what they are afraid of will happen? Why or why not? Discuss these questions in groups.

45. On your own

1. **Imagine that you are a close friend of Blake and Sofia's. You have just received this letter from Sofia. Suggest a solution and explain why you think your solution will have a favorable outcome.**

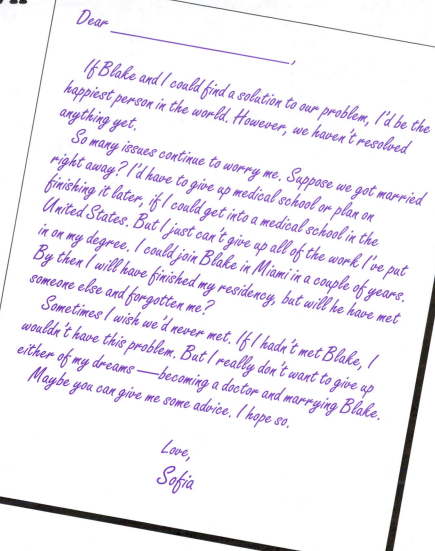

Dear _____,

If Blake and I could find a solution to our problem, I'd be the happiest person in the world. However, we haven't resolved anything yet.

So many issues continue to worry me. Suppose we got married right away? I'd have to give up medical school or plan on finishing it later, if I could get into a medical school in the United States. But I just can't give up all of the work I've put in on my degree. I could join Blake in Miami in a couple of years. By then I will have finished my residency, but will he have met someone else and forgotten me?

Sometimes I wish we'd never met. If I hadn't met Blake, I wouldn't have this problem. But I really don't want to give up either of my dreams —becoming a doctor and marrying Blake. Maybe you can give me some advice. I hope so.

Love,

Sofia

2. **Write an essay about a personal situation in which you are, or were, faced with a variety of choices.**

PREVIEW

FUNCTIONS/THEMES	LANGUAGE	FORMS
Talk about feelings	What do you think of Leslie? I think she's nice, and I appreciate her always being so frank. But I'm getting tired of her teasing me about my diet.	Infinitives with subjects vs. gerunds with subjects
Complain about someone Talk about likes and dislikes	I just can't stand being talked about behind my back. I don't like to be talked about either.	
Complain to someone Give an evaluation	Not only don't you help me around the house, but you also don't help me with the kids. I'm tired of your assuming that I'll do everything. The Wakefield Little Theater either wants to lose money, or it has the worst luck in the history of local theater groups.	*Either . . . or, neither . . . nor,* and *not only . . . but (also)*

Preview the reading.

1. Work with a partner. Would you like to be a famous actor or singer? How do you think your life would be different?

2. Before you read the article on pages 100–101, look at the photos. What words would you use to describe Julio Iglesias? Discuss your ideas with a partner.

Julio Iglesias:
Spanish Prince of Song

1 He is the most popular singer in the world today, and the most popular Spanish singer in history. Since 1968, when he began his professional career, he has sold more than 180 million albums. His face is recognized everywhere, from Moscow to Buenos Aires, and he sings and records in seven languages. He is Julio Iglesias, and in any language his melodic, romantic ballads and warm style appeal to people of all ages and cultures, from Japanese teenagers to Cuban grandmothers.

2 His fans know him as the "Spanish prince of song," but in interviews Iglesias seems relaxed and unassuming. Underneath his natural humility, however, is a driving ambition and an obsession with meeting new challenges. "Let me tell you a story," he says. He is sitting next to one of three swimming pools at his Florida mansion. "You see my house—the swimming pools, the manicured lawn, the Rolls Royce, my success as you put it. When I was finishing this house, I was very happy. But when the house was done, I suddenly got very depressed. And now I know why. It was simply that everything had been finished. What makes my life meaningful is the feeling that I'm actively doing something, that I'm being challenged and my work is never complete."

3 The challenges have not always been in the arena of music. Before he became a singer, Iglesias was living in Spain and playing for a Madrid soccer team. Then, at age 23, he was nearly killed in a car crash that left him paralyzed from the waist down. Doctors predicted he would never walk again, but during three years of intensive rehabilitation he went from wiggling his toes to crawling to walking with crutches, and finally to walking unaided.

4 Iglesias talks of that experience as a turning point in his life. "It's all about making a disadvantage an advantage. I couldn't move, so I opened my eyes more, I listened more, I was more alert for signs, smells, thoughts, and motivations. I discovered I could play a little guitar, I could write something, how to put the songs and the words together."

5 After his recovery, Iglesias went to a local Spanish music festival, submitted a song, and won an award. Almost overnight, he went from being an unknown to being a star.

6 Today, Iglesias is often on tour, traveling from country to country. His proficiency with different languages, while an essential part of his worldwide acceptance, sometimes causes him problems. "It's often very tiring because I not only have to think in a particular language," he says, "but also think whom I'm singing for. Something the French get excited over, a special inflection in your voice, may leave the Japanese completely cold or make them laugh hysterically."

7 But the fact remains that Iglesias is fundamentally Spanish. "I know what I represent for the Spanish world," he says with pride and absolute assurance. "As a singer, I am a leader."

8 In his songwriting, too, he is completely Spanish. "I write only in Spanish. My lyrics are stories that are very simple, common, even naive. These songs come out like a conversation you might have with someone on the street. It's musical talk. I sing the little stories between couples in the world. That is, perhaps, my success in my own language—capturing the intimate *historias.*"

9 Until the early 1980s, most North Americans had never heard of Julio Iglesias, but since then he has put out a number of albums in English, all of them highly successful. After his second all-English album was released, his concert schedule included appearances with Placido Domingo, Charles Aznavour, and Zubin Mehta at Lincoln Center in

Julio Iglesias in concert.

Iglesias playing soccer.

New York City. At one point he had six albums—English and Spanish—on the charts in the United States.

10 His international triumphs have been even greater, as a single example will show: His album *Momentos*, released in Spanish, French, and Italian versions, became the number-one album in ninety countries!

11 As special representative for the performing arts for UNICEF, Iglesias has traveled around the world to perform in fund-raising concerts and to meet with underprivileged children. This aspect of his career holds deep meaning for him. "The world has given me so much," he says. "I am able to live my life in song, and my work with UNICEF is, in a small way, my way of repaying my debt."

12 When asked whether his astounding success makes it hard for him to separate Julio Iglesias the public person from Julio Iglesias the human being, he answers: "I can't separate my life from what I represent or what I do. When I go on stage, of course I get dressed and put on a tie, but the blood runs in my body—I don't fake anything. I'm a natural. And I'm a natural because I don't know how to do any other thing. I know I have talent enough to make people believe I am something else. And I have the talent to sing. I am a singer for sure."

Iglesias signing autographs.

Figure it out

1. **Read the article. Was your description of Julio Iglesias in item 2 on page 99 correct? If necessary, change your description.**

2. **When you have finished reading, decide which of the sentences below describe Julio Iglesias as he is presented in the article. Say *Right* or *Wrong* for each one. If your answer is *Right* find at least one statement in the article that supports it.**

1. His music appeals only to older people.
2. He is hardworking and enjoys a challenge.
3. He speaks more than one language.
4. He is nervous and impatient.
5. He is self-confident about his music.

3. **Iglesias uses the pronoun *it* in a number of his quotes in a way that implies, rather than states, what the pronoun refers to. Explain what you think each highlighted use of *it* listed below refers to.**

1. paragraph 2
2. paragraph 4
3. paragraph 6
4. paragraph 8

4. **Do the statements below accurately state the main purpose of the paragraphs? Say *Right* or *Wrong* for each one, and correct the wrong statements.**

1. Paragraph 1 is about Iglesias's involvement in sports.
2. Paragraphs 3 and 4 are about a non-musical challenge in Iglesias's life.
3. Paragraph 6 is about problems Iglesias sometimes encounters when singing for audiences from different countries.
4. Paragraph 11 describes Iglesias's home.

5. **The suffix *-y* may be added to many words to form nouns. When forming nouns from adjectives, a final *t* or *te* often changes to *c* when the *-y* suffix is added. Form nouns from the adjectives below.**

1. proficient
2. private
3. accurate
4. illiterate
5. vacant
6. urgent

47. I'm sick and tired of his snapping at me.

1. Tell your partner about something you are sick and tired of, and say what you are going to do about it.

Michelle, an aspiring singer, is talking to the band leader, Ray, after a run-in with Kyle, the band's drummer.

Listen to the conversation.

2

Ray What's wrong, Michelle? You look as if you're going to either cry or scream.

Michelle It's Kyle. He really infuriates me. Either he starts acting differently or I'm going to quit. I'm sick and tired of his snapping at me.

Ray What happened this time?

Michelle Well, just now, I couldn't help thinking he was misinterpreting the music. So I made a suggestion, politely, of course.

Ray And?

Michelle Well, not only didn't he take my suggestion, but he interrupted me in the middle of a sentence. He told me to stop complaining and mind my own business. I was only trying to be helpful, and I didn't appreciate being talked to that way.

Ray It sounds to me as if he has trouble accepting criticism.

Michelle Well, nobody likes to be criticized, but I still expect to be treated with some respect.

Ray Maybe it's none of my business, but I'd suggest that you take it up with Kyle directly.

Michelle You're absolutely right. There's no point in my wasting time complaining behind Kyle's back.

Ray I agree. But at the same time, I don't think you should worry about it too much. You need to focus all your energy on our next concert. You know how important that concert is to us. And it's a big opportunity for you.

Michelle You're right. I guess I just have to learn not to take these things so seriously.

3. Check (√) the statements that are stated or implied in the conversation.

_____ 1. Michelle and Kyle have had problems before.

_____ 2. Kyle is very easygoing.

_____ 3. Kyle criticized the way Michelle was singing.

_____ 4. Kyle doesn't like to be criticized.

_____ 5. Michelle and Ray get along well.

_____ 6. Ray gives Michelle advice on how to handle the situation.

_____ 7. Ray offers to help by talking to Kyle.

_____ 8. Michelle isn't really upset at all.

48. I have to learn not to take things so seriously.

1 ▶ **Listen to the conversation.**
   ▶ **Act out similar conversations. Tell your partner what you like and don't like about the people in the box.**

A What do you think of Leslie?
B Well, I think she's nice and I appreciate her always being so frank. But I'm getting tired of her teasing me about my diet.
A Maybe you should say something to her.
B Hmm . . . I doubt it would do any good. I guess I just have to learn not to take things so seriously.

Some people

Leslie is nice, but she is extremely frank. Also, she often teases people about personal things.
Arturo is very smart and he knows something about every subject. However, he dominates every conversation.
Patricia works hard and she is always busy trying to get ahead. However, she's never on time for anything.
Jeff is a nice guy and he tries to be a good friend. However, he's always telling everyone what to do.

2 ▶ **Listen to David talk about some people where he works. For each behavior listed below, write the name of the person David talks about. If David doesn't mention a name, write X.**

_____ ignores him at meetings.
_____ talks about him behind his back.
_____ criticizes his work.
_____ teases him about his car.
_____ yells at him for being late.

Some expressions

I admire . . .
I appreciate . . .
I'm (sick and) tired of . . .
I dislike . . .

I can't stand . . .
I (don't) like . . .

◀ + gerund

◀ + infinitive or gerund

When these expressions are followed by a pronoun and a gerund, the pronoun is a *possessive* pronoun.
   I appreciate *his* being frank.

3 ▶ **Study the frames: Infinitives with subjects vs. gerunds with subjects**

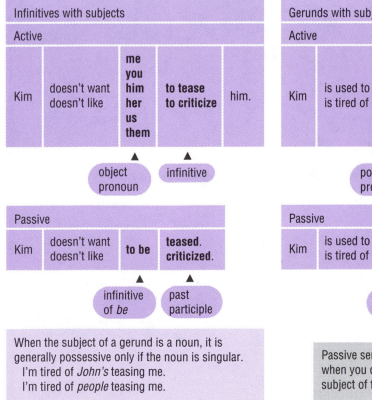

Infinitives with subjects
Active

Kim	doesn't want / doesn't like	me you him her us them	to tease to criticize	him.
		▲ object pronoun	▲ infinitive	

Passive

Kim	doesn't want / doesn't like	to be	teased. criticized.
		▲ infinitive of *be*	▲ past participle

Gerunds with subjects
Active

Kim	is used to / is tired of	my your his her our their	teasing criticizing	him.
		▲ possessive pronoun	▲ gerund	

Passive

Kim	is used to / is tired of	being	teased. criticized.
		▲ gerund of *be*	▲ past participle

When the subject of a gerund is a noun, it is generally possessive only if the noun is singular.
   I'm tired of *John's* teasing me.
   I'm tired of *people* teasing me.

Passive sentences are generally used when you do not want to express the subject of the infinitive or gerund.

4 ► Listen to the conversation.

► Act out similar conversations with a partner. Imagine that you are upset because someone has done one of the things in the box to you. Tell your partner what's wrong.

A What's wrong?

B Oh, nothing. I just can't stand being talked about behind my back.

A I don't like to be talked about, either, but I think it's worse if you don't do anything about it.

B What do you mean?

A Maybe it's none of my business, but I'd suggest that you take it up with the person directly.

Has someone . . .
talked about you behind your back?
insulted you to your face?
asked you personal questions about your finances?
yelled at you for no reason?
ignored you?
laughed at you?

5 ► Rewrite what these performers said about their work, combining the sentences in brackets [ ] into one sentence that contains an infinitive or gerund with a subject.

We asked some performers what they love and hate about their work.

1. Directors can be very impatient and very sensitive. [They yell at me in front of everyone else. I especially don't like that.]

2. Writers often seem indecisive. [They change our lines. I get tired of that.]

3. Our music is very different. It's a completely new sound. [People sometimes criticize our music when they don't understand it. I don't appreciate that.]

4. It's nice to be recognized in public. [People ask me for my autograph. I really like that.]

5. I used to work on stage, but now I'm in television. [The audience applauds after a performance. I miss that.]

6 ► Work with a partner. Talk about your situation at work, home, or school. Say what you like and don't like, using some of the expressions in the box.

I really like	being . . . to be . . .
I don't like	being . . . to be . . .
I get tired of	people . . . my boss's . . . my classmates/coworkers . . .
I appreciate	my teacher's . . . my relatives . . . people . . .

7 ▶ **Listen to the conversation.**
 ▶ **Act out similar conversations. You are unhappy about one of the situations in the box. Complain to your partner, who will play the role of the person you're angry with.**

A Oscar, can I talk to you for a second?
B Sure. What is it?
A Well, not only don't you help me around the house, but you also don't help me with the kids. It really infuriates me. I'm tired of your assuming that I'll do everything.
B I'm sorry. Why didn't you say so before? I didn't realize you wanted help.

> Compare the order of the words in italics.
> Not only *don't you* help around the house, but *you don't* help with the kids.

> **Some situations**
>
> Your spouse doesn't help you around the house. What's more, he or she doesn't help you with the kids. Your spouse assumes you will do everything and you're tired of it.
> An employee of yours is always late for work. What's more, the employee never apologizes when he or she finally arrives. You don't like the fact that the employee treats the job so casually.
> A coworker always comes back from lunch late. What's more, he or she always leaves work early. You think it's unfair that you always have to make excuses for your coworker and finish his or her work.
> Your brother or sister is always listening to your phone conversations. What's more, he or she is always opening your mail. You really don't appreciate it.

8 ▶ **Study the frames:**
 Either . . . or, neither . . . nor, **and** *not only . . . but (also)*

| Jim must be tired. *If not, then* he's angry. |
| Jane didn't call, *and* she didn't come to work. |
| Tim is a snob. *What's more*, he's a bore. |

▶

Jim's	**either**	tired	**or**	angry.
Jane	**neither**	called	**nor**	came to work.
Tim's	**not only**	a snob	**but (also)**	a bore.

> **Emphatic word order**
>
> Jane neither called nor *did she come* to work.
> Not only *is Tim* a snob, but he's also a bore.

> When these conjunctions connect two subjects or two complete sentences, a conjunction starts the sentence.
> *Neither* Jim *nor* Jane called him.
> *Either* the director apologizes *or* I'm going to quit.

9 ▶ **Rewrite the play review, combining the sentences in brackets [ ] into one sentence using *either . . . or, neither . . . nor,* or *not only . . . but (also)*.**

A DISGRACE FROM BEGINNING TO END

by Kent Brownridge

[The Wakefield Little Theater must want to lose money. If not, then it has the worst luck in the history of local theater groups.] [Its last production was terrible. What's more, its current one, *Out Back*, is just as bad.] Although *Out Back* is billed as a "hilarious new musical," [it's not a musical and it's not a comedy.] [A lot of the actors are amateurish. If not, then they're badly cast,] and the few songs they sing out of tune are far from humorous.

Moreover, the play is not the only disgrace. The theater itself is a disgrace. [It is run-down. What's more, it is uncomfortable.] I have only one piece of advice for this theater: [Shape up immediately. If not, then close down.] There is no reason for a theater to have one bad production after another, and I would not be at all surprised if the theater is half empty at its next performance.

49. Your turn

1. Read the descriptions of the three men and three women. Then, working in groups, decide which people would be happiest together as married couples. Match each person with a partner.

2. Now work with a partner and discuss two of the people who you did not think would make a happily married couple. Imagine that they are married and discuss the problems they are having living together. Try to find a solution to their disagreements.

Edmund is an engineer who is independent and climbing rapidly in his field. He wants to marry and start a family. He spends more time at work than anywhere else.

🎞 Listen in

One of the people in the pictures is complaining to a friend about his wife. Read the questions below. Then listen to the conversation and answer the questions.

1. Who do you think the husband and wife are? Why?
2. The friend started to offer some advice. What do you think she was going to suggest?

Ellen is a secretary who is easygoing and not ambitious. She doesn't expect to work after having children, and she isn't interested in material things. She's very sensitive.

Derek is an accountant who likes to take charge of things. He has traditional views on male–female roles in marriage. He's very critical and ambitious.

Victor is an actor who is a pleasant, likeable person with a strong wish to help others. Unfortunately, he's often out of work and doesn't make much money.

Hilda is a lawyer who is independent and intellectual. She's not sure if she wants to get married, and she strongly wants to pursue her career. She is a tolerant person, but not outgoing.

Natalie is a professor who is conservative, ambitious, materialistic, critical, and family-oriented. She admires hard work.

50. On your own

1. **Read the following advertisements. Then write an advertisement of your own, explaining your requirements for a roommate, traveling companion, or partner for some activity you enjoy.**

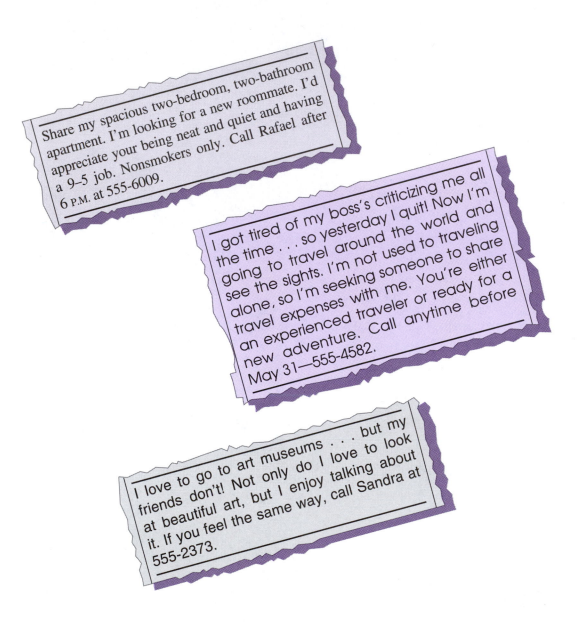

Share my spacious two-bedroom, two-bathroom apartment. I'm looking for a new roommate. I'd appreciate your being neat and quiet and having a 9–5 job. Nonsmokers only. Call Rafael after 6 P.M. at 555-6009.

I got tired of my boss's criticizing me all the time . . . so yesterday I quit! Now I'm going to travel around the world and see the sights. I'm not used to traveling alone, so I'm seeking someone to share travel expenses with me. You're either an experienced traveler or ready for a new adventure. Call anytime before May 31—555-4582.

I love to go to art museums . . . but my friends don't! Not only do I love to look at beautiful art, but I enjoy talking about it. If you feel the same way, call Sandra at 555-2373.

2. **Write about a problem or disagreement that you either had in the past or have now with someone—for example, a boss, a spouse, or a friend. First, describe the problem and your feelings about it. Then, explain what you did or are going to do about the situation and why.**

PREVIEW

FUNCTIONS/THEMES	LANGUAGE	FORMS
Speculate about possibilities	You know, I tried to get hold of Mike all weekend, but the phone was always busy. He couldn't have been talking that whole time. Maybe the phone was off the hook. I suppose it might have been.	Short answers with modal auxiliaries
Give a description	We're looking for a red-haired woman who stole a white Toyota. Did you happen to see her? I don't believe so. But I did see a gray-haired woman riding a bike and holding a cat under her arm, which I thought was odd. The woman we're looking for, who we think had on a black skirt, was very tall and she was wearing glasses.	Nonrestrictive vs. restrictive relative clauses
Tell a story React to a story Speculate about possibilities	The Freeman Gallery, which is located in London, sells paintings and other art objects. It seems to me that they must have climbed in through the window.	

Preview the reading.

1. What is the person in the picture below doing? Do you know his name and what he's famous for? Discuss your answers with a partner.

2. Before you read the article on pages 110–111, look at the title and the diagram. What do you think the article is about? Discuss your ideas with a partner.

The Science of Murder

① Painful as it is to think about, murder has become a grim fact of modern society, and solving one involves more than the contributions of the police and witnesses. It also involves the detailed work of people in the fields of forensic science and medicine: scientists and doctors who analyze evidence to help solve murders.

② Forensic science has a colorful history. An early case was the 1849 murder by a chemistry professor of a man who had contributed large sums of money to Harvard University. In that case, pieces of bone and teeth found in the ashes of the professor's laboratory furnace were used in the courtroom as evidence. In 1892, the first murder case that was solved through fingerprint evidence occurred in Argentina, and in 1910, a doctor was found guilty of murdering his wife based on a small piece of skin found in his basement. A scar on that skin was identified as a surgical scar the victim had on her stomach. The doctor was hanged.

③ Today the evidence of forensic scientists ranges from footprints to blood samples, from hair analyses to identification of bite marks. Their work begins at the scene of the crime, and their first piece of evidence is a body—a dead body.

④ Before the body is removed to the morgue, the location of every item in the scene is diagrammed, and then the search is begun for physical evidence that could identify the killer. The killer could have left saliva on a cigarette butt, a good set of fingerprints on a glass, hairs on a hat, or blood from a cut. Once the possible sources of evidence are identified, investigators must be careful to protect them, as all too easily, evidence may be destroyed. If the murderer was smoking a cigarette and threw it in a toilet, the evidence will be gone if someone flushes the toilet. Likewise, if a police officer picks up the telephone at the scene of the crime, the fingerprint evidence may disappear.

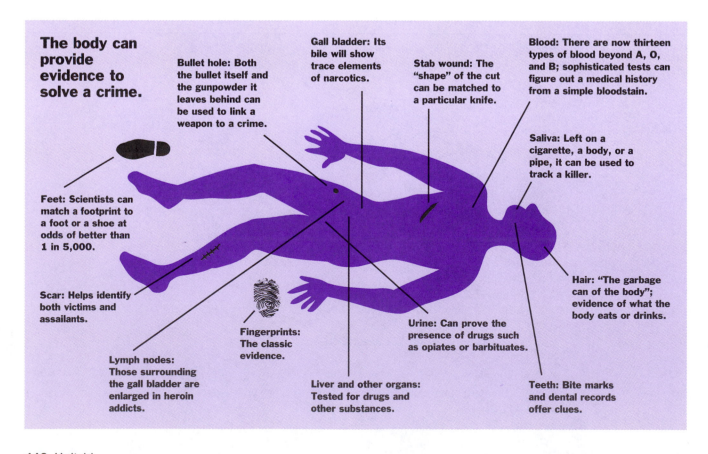

The body can provide evidence to solve a crime.

Bullet hole: Both the bullet itself and the gunpowder it leaves behind can be used to link a weapon to a crime.

Gall bladder: Its bile will show trace elements of narcotics.

Stab wound: The "shape" of the cut can be matched to a particular knife.

Blood: There are now thirteen types of blood beyond A, O, and B; sophisticated tests can figure out a medical history from a simple bloodstain.

Saliva: Left on a cigarette, a body, or a pipe, it can be used to track a killer.

Feet: Scientists can match a footprint to a foot or a shoe at odds of better than 1 in 5,000.

Scar: Helps identify both victims and assailants.

Fingerprints: The classic evidence.

Urine: Can prove the presence of drugs such as opiates or barbituates.

Hair: "The garbage can of the body"; evidence of what the body eats or drinks.

Lymph nodes: Those surrounding the gall bladder are enlarged in heroin addicts.

Liver and other organs: Tested for drugs and other substances.

Teeth: Bite marks and dental records offer clues.

⑤ The next step is the medical examination, and an examiner will arrive at the scene to confirm the death and check the body for injuries. The body will then be shipped to the morgue, where a forensic autopsy will be performed. This involves close examination of both the outside and inside of the body. The specialist will study the hands and face for signs that a fight took place and will remove any evidence, such as a bullet, that is in the body. He or she will also send samples of body organs to the laboratory to see if the victim took any drugs.

⑥ Besides testing the body for evidence, forensic technicians must also analyze all evidence the police have provided from the scene. If the murder involved a shooting, ballistics experts—specialists in firearms and ammunition—will also be involved in the investigation. Using a microscope, they will try to match bullets taken from the scene with any bullet holes found, and they will also try to identify the gun. A gun leaves unique marks on bullets fired from it; in fact, marks on two bullets from the same gun are as alike as two prints from the same finger. In addition, experts will examine any gunpowder found around a bullet hole to see how far away the gun was when it was fired. By examining the gunpowder, they will also try to identify where the gun came from and on what day it was sold.

⑦ It is common knowledge that fingerprints can be traced to an individual person; likewise, footprints can be used. "There are 46 points of measurement and 120 points to examine for shape," says anthropologist Louise Robbins. Footprints can also be found in people's shoes, and scientists like Robbins help the police match a shoe to its wearer.

⑧ Hair, too, can be matched with increasing accuracy. People's hair can differ in color, texture, thickness, and twenty other characteristics. "The hair is the garbage can of the body," says forensic scientist, Dr. Robert Shaler. "Everything you eat shows up there." Since hair grows one millimeter a day, an analysis can tell "if you took aspirin yesterday and drank beer from an aluminum can a week ago."

⑨ Blood type has long been used as evidence. Since 1988 a new kind of evidence, known as DNA fingerprinting, can also be used in court. This method involves matching the genetic material (DNA) of a suspect to genetic material found at the scene of the crime. DNA can be obtained from blood, skin, or hair left by the murderer. This DNA matching has tied hundreds of individuals to their crimes—and has established the innocence of others who were wrongly found guilty before DNA tests were available. DNA matching does not completely eliminate the possibility of mistakes, but it is extremely accurate.

⑩ Murder is a dreadful business indeed, but let the murderer beware. The findings that come out of a forensic scientist's work may be very dramatic and revealing.

Figure it out

1. **Read the first paragraph of the article. Then explain what forensic science is.**

2. **As you read the article, pay attention to the purpose of each paragraph. When you have finished, find the paragraph that . . .**

1. describes the forensic autopsy.
2. describes the initial investigation and discusses the importance of protecting evidence.
3. discusses why hair is useful in solving a murder.
4. gives the history of forensic science.
5. describes what ballistic experts do.
6. explains the importance of DNA tests.

3. **Try to answer the quetions below from memory. Then scan the article again and make any necessary corrections.**

1. What is one way evidence could be destroyed by accident?
2. What is one type of evidence that could be found during the forensic autopsy?
3. What is one thing ballistic experts will try to do?
4. What can an analysis of hair show?
5. What can an analysis of blood show?

4. **The suffixes *-ful* and *-less*, which are opposites, are used to form many adjectives, as in *careful* (with care) and *careless* (without care). Complete the paragraph below, using words from the list.**

careful   fearful   painful   useful
careless   fearless   painless   useless

Crime is spreading to the far reaches of our society, and the _____ fact is that we are doing very little to stop it. It is _____ to simply talk about violence, while people are becoming more and more _____ and suspicious of each other. Unless we are very _____ , the problem is likely to get out of control.

52. This isn't "Murder in Madrid"!

1. You and your partner were supposed to meet your friend Sheila at a restaurant at 8:00. It is now 9:30 and you have just finished eating. Sheila never showed up. What do you think happened to her? Discuss all of the possibilities.

 Jeanette and Tony Huber are looking forward to watching the final episode of "Murder in Madrid" on television.

Listen to the conversation.

(2)

Tony Hey, it's 9:00. Time for "Murder in Madrid."

Jeanette Oh, that's right. Tonight's the final episode. Let me change the channel.

Tony Look, this isn't "Murder in Madrid"!

Jeanette Do you suppose they canceled it?

Tony They couldn't have. Not my favorite program.

Jeanette Well, it must not be on tonight, which is odd.

Tony It has to be. Let me check the TV listings. (*Opens newspaper*) Oh, no, look at this! "Due to special programming, the final episode of 'Murder in Madrid' will be shown next week at this time." It seems the Academy of Music awards are on instead.

Jeanette I can't believe it! Now we'll have to wait a week to find out who the murderer was.

Tony Listen, don't worry. Look what I bought.

Jeanette *Murder in Madrid?* You bought the book?

Tony I hear it's even better than the series, which is why I wanted to read it. But now I can look at the end and find out what happens.

Jeanette Oh, Tony, you wouldn't!

Tony Why not? I'm dying to know who killed Ackerman . . . and that woman in the nightclub, who I thought was the best one in the series.

Jeanette As long as you don't tell *me* who did it. I can wait until next week.

Tony Well, I can't. But don't worry. My lips are sealed.

Jeanette They'd better be.

Tony (*Opens book and starts to read*) Oh, no . . . she couldn't have. She was only . . . Jeanette, you won't believe this. . . .

Jeanette Tony! Come on! I don't want to hear it.

Tony What's wrong with reading the book before you see the end? You're so conventional.

Jeanette Maybe I am. In any case, I *don't* want to know what happened!

3. Match.

1. They're showing the Academy of Music awards instead of "Murder in Madrid."
2. Do you suppose they canceled the show?
3. It must not be on tonight.
4. Don't tell me who did it.
5. I can wait until next week.
6. You're so conventional.

a. It has to be.
b. Maybe I am.
c. They can't be.
d. Well, I can't.
e. They couldn't have. Not my favorite program.
f. Don't worry. I won't.

53. Maybe the phone was off the hook.

  1 ▶ **Listen to two police officers talk about a crime. Check (√) the picture that shows what they think happened.**

 2 ▶ **Listen to the conversation.**
▶ **Act out similar conversations with a partner. You are puzzled about one of the situations in the box. Your partner will help you come up with a possible explanation.**

A You know, I tried to get hold of Mike all weekend, but the phone was always busy. He couldn't have been talking that whole time.
B Maybe the phone was off the hook.
A I suppose it might have been. Either that or it was out of order.

> Compare these short answers.
> *It might have been* (off the hook).
> *He might have* (taken it off the hook).

> **Some situations**
>
> You tried to get hold of Mike all weekend, but the phone was always busy. You know he couldn't have been talking that whole time.
> Maria had promised to call you tonight, but she didn't. You were going to get together. You wonder what happened.
> You got a vase in the mail today, but you don't know who it was from. You didn't buy it, and there was no name or address on the package.
> You went over to Glen's after work, but no one was home. He knew you were coming, and you can't imagine why he wasn't there.

3 ▶ **Study the frames: Short answers with modal auxiliaries**

With forms of *be*		Without forms of *be*	
Maybe Eva's still at work.	**She can't be.**	Try to remember the robber.	**I can't.**
Do you think she's sleeping?	**She might be.**	I hope the police find him.	**They might not.**
Was Eva at home?	**She must not have been.**	Has Lee called the police?	**He must have.**
Was she expecting us?	**She should have been.**	Did he change the door lock?	**He should have.**

> When the complete sentence contains a form of *be*, the form of *be* is part of the short answer.
> She might *be* sleeping. → She might *be*.
> She must not have *been* at home. → She might not have *been*.

4 ▶ **It's closing time and Hiro and Yoko Otani, who own a small stationery store, have just noticed that their cash box is missing. Complete their conversation, choosing the correct modal auxiliaries in parentheses.**

Yoko Try to think of someplace we haven't looked.
Hiro I _____ (can't/couldn't/can't be). We've looked everywhere.
Yoko Well, I guess it was stolen then.
Hiro It _____ (will have been/must have been/must be). But I can't figure out how.
Yoko There were lots of people in here today. Do you remember if it was locked up?

Hiro It _____ (couldn't have been/should have/should have been), but perhaps Linda or Ken left it out by mistake. Do you think they're home yet? It's 5:45.
Yoko They _____ (will be/might not be/might not), but I could try calling them.
Hiro O.K. Maybe you'd better call the police, too.
Yoko I _____ (will/shouldn't/should have), but first I want to speak to Linda and Ken.

5 ▶ **Listen to the conversation.**

▶ **Act out similar conversations with a partner. Imagine you are a police officer who is questioning bystanders about several incidents. Your partner will play the role of the bystander and describe what he or she saw.**

A Excuse me, sir. We're looking for a red-haired woman who stole a white Toyota from Dan's Parking Lot a few minutes ago. Did you happen to see her?

B I don't believe so. But I did see a gray-haired woman riding a bike and holding a cat under her arm, which I thought was odd.

A The woman we're looking for, who we think had on a black skirt, was very tall and she was wearing glasses. . . .

> Compare:
> This woman, *who* . . .
> This dog, *which* . . .

The police officer is looking for . . .
a red-haired woman who stole a white Toyota from Dan's Parking Lot. She was very tall and she was wearing glasses. She probably had on a black skirt.
a little boy with a baseball bat who broke the window at Sims' bakery. He was wearing shorts and he had on a baseball hat. He probably had blond hair.
a large dog that bit a man on the ankle. It was black and it had a white spot on its tail. It probably was wearing a leather collar.
a young man who walked out of Friendly Appliance Store with an electric iron under his raincoat. He was very heavy and he had a mustache. He was probably in his early twenties.

The bystander saw . . .
a gray-haired woman riding a bike and holding a cat under her arm. It was an odd sight.
a little girl wearing a football uniform and carrying a tennis racket. It was an unusual sight.
a striped cat chasing a butterfly down the street. It was a funny sight.
a young woman walk into Friendly Appliance Store with four toasters in her arms. It was a strange sight.

6 ▶ **Study the frames: Nonrestrictive vs. restrictive relative clauses**

Nonrestrictive relative clauses					
Relative pronouns as subjects			Relative pronouns as objects		
Amy Bing,	**who**	**looks so nice,**	stole a car.	That's Mr. Smith,	**who(m)**	**I told you about.**
That dog,	**which**	**is very mean,**	once bit me.	I miss my old car,	**which**	**I sold.**

Sometimes a relative pronoun may take the place of a subject or an object that is a whole clause or sentence.
  "Murder in Madrid" must not be on tonight, which is really odd.
  (Which = the fact that "Murder in Madrid" must not be on.)
	Whom is used when the relative pronoun is an object.
	  I told you about *him* (Mr. Smith).
	  That's Mr. Smith, *whom* I told you about.
	In everyday speech, *who* can also be used in these cases.

Nonrestrictive vs. restrictive relative clauses	
Nonrestrictive clauses	Restrictive clauses

A nonrestrictive clause gives information that is *not* essential in order to identify the subject or object it refers to. Therefore, the clause is set off by commas.
  That dog, which is very mean, once bit me.
  That's Mr. Smith, who(m) you once met.
	A restrictive clause gives information that *is* essential in order to identify the subject or object it refers to. Therefore, the clause is not set off by commas.
	  The dog that bit me belongs to my neighbor.
	  The man who(m) you met at my house is my boss.

The pronouns *who* and *whom* are used to refer to people, and the pronoun *which* is used to refer to things.	The pronouns *who*, *whom*, and *that* are used to refer to people, and the pronoun *that* is used to refer to things.

7 ▶ **Millicent Berger, a famous mystery writer, is working out the plot for her latest book, *A Matter of Murder*. Rewrite her notes, combining each pair of sentences in brackets [ ] into one sentence with either a nonrestrictive or a restrictive relative clause.**

Start like this:

The Freeman Gallery, which is located in London, sells paintings and other art objects. . . .

[The Freeman Gallery sells paintings and other art objects. It is located in London.] [Mr. Baldwin is the manager. He has two assistants, Ms. Farkas and Mr. Kumar.] Downstairs there is a gallery and a sales office. [Upstairs is Mr. Baldwin's office. This is where the money is kept.] On Saturday at 12:00, Mr. Baldwin and his assistants were at work in the gallery. [Sally Dupont came to the gallery and tried unsuccessfully to get Mr. Baldwin to exhibit her paintings. Mr. Baldwin dislikes her.] [Mr. Baldwin left the gallery at 12:15. He usually walks home for lunch.] [Mr. Kumar offered to take Sally Dupont to a gallery. The gallery probably would agree to exhibit her work.] They left at 12:20. [Ms. Farkas said she was going to put away the money. The gallery had made the money that morning.] Before she left for lunch, she locked up the gallery. [Mr. Baldwin came back unexpectedly at 12:40. He usually returns at 1:00.] [Mr. Kumar returned at 1:00 and couldn't open the door. It was locked.] Ms. Farkas returned at 1:05 and unlocked the door. They found Mr. Baldwin dead. Police say he was shot at approximately 12:45. After finding an angry letter from Sally Dupont in Mr. Baldwin's desk, the police arrested her for the murder.

8 ▶ **Now discuss Millicent Berger's notes with a partner. Do you think the police arrested the right person? Why or why not? Who do *you* think killed Mr. Baldwin? What do you think happened?**

9 ▶ **Imagine that one of the items mentioned in the box was stolen from you. Work in small groups and try to figure out what happened to it.**

A *All they took is the Picasso, which I think is pretty strange. What's more, I can't figure out how they got in here.*

B *It seems to me they must have climbed in through the window. After all, it was open.*

A *They couldn't have. Someone definitely would have seen them.*

C *Well, it had to be someone who knew you had the painting. Is there any possibility that . . . ?*

Some situations

You came home and found that a window was open. Your valuable Picasso painting was missing, but nothing else was taken. Your apartment faces the street, and it was still light out.

You are a history professor. Two days before final exams, one copy of the exam disappeared from your desk. You always lock your office door, but not your desk drawer, when you leave the office.

You are a lawyer attending a conference with the president of your company. While you were taking a shower, your briefcase, which contained confidential papers concerning your company's finances, was taken from your room. Your wallet and watch were not taken.

Some expressions

It seems to me (that) . . .
(Who) do you suppose . . . ?
Is there any possibility (that) . . . ?
It seems unlikely (that) . . . ?
It couldn't have been . . .

54. Your turn

Study the pictures carefully, and then work in groups to develop a plot for *Murder at the Villa*, a new murder mystery. Give each character a name and make notes about the personality and background of each one. When developing your story, consider these questions.

1. Which one of the characters was killed? Was more than one person murdered?
2. What was the motive for the murder?
3. How was the murder committed? What evidence was found at the scene?
4. Which of the characters committed the crime?

🔊 Listen in

1. **A police officer and a police sergeant are discussing the crime. Read the question below. Then listen to the conversation and answer the question.**

What evidence did the police officer find, and where did he find it?

2. **How is the information in the conversation you just heard different from the information in your plot? Discuss this question in your group.**

a bottle
of poison

a plant

a hypodermic
needle

a bottle
of wine

55. On your own

1. Choose one of the options below.

1. Write an account of your group's version of *Murder at the Villa*.
2. Write a short summary of a real mystery, such as a book you read or a movie you saw recently. Include what happened, how it happened, who did it, and why.

2. Think about a well-known crime that happened recently. Write a newspaper account, including as many details as possible.

FAMOUS PAINTING STOLEN

The modern art masterpiece "Exile," which was painted by Venezuelan artist Mariluz Calderón in 1973, has disappeared from the Patton Museum. Police speculate that it was stolen sometime early Saturday morning.

Investigators are looking for clues throughout the international art world. When asked if the motive for the theft was money, Police Chief Edward Singer said, "It must have been. We think the thieves will try to sell the painting, which our experts tell us is worth over one million dollars."

Police search the scene of the crime for clues after discovering the theft of the modern art masterpiece "Exile" Saturday morning.

FUNCTIONS/THEMES	LANGUAGE	FORMS

Talk about preferences
Respond tactfully
	Do you like modern dance?
	Actually, I'm not all that crazy about it.
	  What I really like is folk dancing.
	There's a new exhibit of fifteenth-century
	  Italian paintings at the museum. Maybe
	  we ought to go there sometime.
	That might be interesting, but modern art is
	  what I really like.
		Special word order for emphasis

Give opinions	That sounds good, but what I'd really like to see sometime is an opera.	

Respond tactfully	There's nothing wrong with innovative
	  styles, yet I'm personally more comfortable
	  with a conservative look.
	Well, you might like it once you get used
	  to it.	

Give a reaction	I love opera, whereas/while my husband
	  can't stand it. He said he'd rather listen to
	  a cat fight.
	How did you react when he said that?
	I just laughed it off.
		Connectors *in spite of* and *despite;*
		yet; nevertheless and *nonetheless;*
		whereas and *while;* and *however*
		and *on the other hand*

Preview the reading.

1. Work with a partner. Discuss the different kinds of dances in the pictures below. Talk about the kinds of dances you like to watch and the kinds you like to do.

2. Before you read the article on pages 120–121, look at the title and the photos. Discuss with your partner what you think the article will tell you about Martha Graham.

Martha Graham:
A SYNONYM FOR MODERN DANCE

by Anna Kisselgoff

The name Martha Graham is practically a synonym for the art form known as modern dance, which dates from her pioneering days as a dancer and a choreographer in the late 1920s. Often seen as a rebellion against the 350-year-old tradition of classical ballet, modern dance is the world's

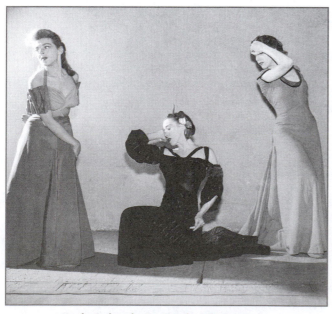

Martha Graham dancing "Primitive Mysteries."

Martha Graham dancing "Deaths and Entrances."

first lasting alternative to that tradition. Graham has rightly been called a genius and one of the greatest artists the United States has ever produced. When she died in 1991, at age 96, of heart failure following pneumonia, the dance world went into mourning.

Change was a major factor throughout Graham's career. In the early 1920s, Graham came to feel that the radical changes brought by World War I required a new and different style of dance. After attending a famous dance school in California called Denishawn, she and two other dancers made a dramatic break from the Denishawn dance company. In 1927, a reporter for the *New York Times* coined the term "Modern Dance" to describe their new and innovative style.

Graham's early dances of the 1930s were stark and simple; these contrast with the poetic theater pieces of the 1940s and even more sharply with the complex dance-dramas based on Greek mythology that characterized the 1950s and 1960s. In these, several performers would each portray different aspects of the same character's personality. Often, scenes from the past, present, and future would occur at the same time, making it impossible to distinguish clearly one period of time from another. Graham's later work, on the other hand, tended to be less complex. "The absolute thing is now," she said once. "Change is the only constant."

Yet, despite these changes, Graham always remained true to a basic belief that dance expresses emotion we often try to hide and cannot express in words. "I don't want to be understandable," she declared. "I want to be felt." Indeed, people who saw her dances often spoke of feeling enormously moved by what they didn't truly understand. As a child in Allegheny, Pennsylvania, Graham made a discovery that she later saw as related to her belief in the importance of expressing hidden emotion. One day her father invited her to look through a microscope. "My father," she recalled, "asked, 'What does it look like?' 'Water,' I said, 'clear water.' 'Yes, but what kind?' he asked. I said, 'There are wriggles in it.' And he said, 'Yes, it's impure. You must look for truth below the surface.'" Graham's dances are open to many interpretations, and like abstract painters, she invites the viewer to bring his or her emotions to the work, to complete the picture. She remembers being influenced by Wassily Kandinsky when, as a young woman, she happened to see a painting of his—a slash of red against a field of blue—and decided, "I will dance like that."

Graham also focused throughout her career on certain themes. The theme of rebirth, for example, was a central one for her. This theme is evident in the dramatic series of falls to the floor that Graham invented, in which the dancer seems to sink backward. Graham described the fall as "a spring up to life." Another theme is that of defiance and conformity, as expressed in the early dance, "Heretic," in which a group of dancers in gray reject and punish a single dancer in white because she is different. Graham was also interested in themes of ritual, sexuality, and death. All her themes related ultimately to her desire to explore the human spirit.

Will Martha Graham's influence survive her? The answer is almost certainly yes. First of all, there is her repertoire of over 180 dances; second, the Martha Graham Dance Company continues to tour the United States and the world under the successors she picked; third, many of today's leading choreographers were once members of her dance company and acknowledge their debt to Martha Graham. But perhaps the most important reason her work will last is that she so successfully mixed her themes with her individuality and with self-discovery. Although her message is universal, her work is distinctive because, as she said, "It has to come from one person's experience. I have never been able to divorce the dancing from life."

Martha Graham, rehearsing a dancer to perform "Heretic" with the Martha Graham Dance Company.

Figure it out

1. **As you read the article, pay attention to the examples the author uses to support what she feels are Martha Graham's main ideas on dance. When you have finished, say which of the main ideas (*a, b,* or *c*) the author has tried to illustrate with each of the examples below.**

   a. Change is essential. Everything cannot always remain the same.
   b. Dance appeals to the viewer's hidden emotions, which are hard to express in words, and is open to more than one interpretation.
   c. Dance, like life with its rises and falls, is a continuous cycle of rebirth.

   1. Graham's early dance "Heretic."
   2. Graham's dramatic series of falls.
   3. The differences in the style of Graham's work over the years.
   4. Wassily Kandinsky's painting and her father's lesson.

2. **Now look at a few of Martha Graham's quotes from the article, and say which main idea listed in exercise 1 you think each quote expresses most closely.**

   1. "I don't want to be understandable. I want to be felt."
   2. "You must look for the truth below the surface."
   3. "The absolute thing is now. Change is the only constant."

3. **The suffixes *-able*, as in *understandable*, and *-ive*, as in *innovative*, are used to form many adjectives. Complete the sentences below by changing the verbs in parentheses to adjectives ending in either *-able* or *-ive*. Use your dictionary if necessary.**

   1. There are still many people who find classical ballet _____ (prefer) to modern dance.
   2. Juana is extremely _____ (create). She's written three novels.
   3. Nothing is more _____ (enjoy) than a relaxing day at the beach.
   4. The Stones are too _____ (overprotect) of their children. They should let them be more _____ (act).

57. What I really like is...

1. Praise something that you like very much, such as a kind of music, a musical group, an artist, a book, or a kind of food, and ask your partner how he or she likes it. Your partner should answer honestly. If your partner's preferences are different, he or she should try to respond without hurting your feelings.

 Rita has two tickets to see the Pilobolus Dance Theater, and she invites her friend Rick to go with her.

Listen to the conversation.

Rita I have two tickets to see the Pilobolus Dance Theater on Saturday. Would you like to go with me?

Rick Is that a ballet company? I love ballet.

Rita Well, this is more innovative. It combines mime, dance, and acrobatics.

Rick That sounds interesting, but do you think I'd enjoy it? What I really like is classical ballet.

Rita Well, as I said, this isn't ballet, yet it's so entertaining that I think you would like it.

Rick You're right. I don't want to sound like my brother Fred did at a ballet once.

Rita Why, what happened?

Rick Oh, it's just that I sat there spellbound, whereas *he* fell asleep. All he had to say afterwards was, "They looked like a bunch of frogs hopping around in nightgowns."

Rita Weren't you insulted?

Rick No, I just laughed it off. Fred's always been tactless. But I'll be glad to go with you to see this other group.

Rita Good. And we can have dinner at that new Tex-Mex place.

Rick What's that?

Rita It's the kind of Mexican food they make in southern Texas. It's pretty spicy, because they use lots of chile peppers.

Rick Hmm . . . Well, I guess it wouldn't hurt to give it a try. Traditional American food is what I prefer—you know, hamburgers and french fries—but I suppose it's good to try new things every once in a while.

3. Say *Tactful* or *Tactless*.

1. The Pilobolus Dance Theater sounds interesting, but what I really like is classical ballet.
2. I really can't stand Tex-Mex food.
3. Ballet dancers look like a bunch of frogs hopping around in nightgowns.
4. I guess it wouldn't hurt to give it a try.
5. Actually, ballet isn't my favorite kind of dance. Flamenco dancing is what I really love.

58. That might be interesting, but...

 1 ▶ **Listen to the two possible conversations.**
   ▶ **Act out similar conversations with a partner. Give your true opinions.**

A Do you like modern dance?

B Yes, I do. In fact, the dance group I like best is Pilobolus.

B Actually, I'm not all that crazy about it. What I really like is folk dancing.

Do you like . . .	
modern dance?	science fiction?
ballet?	rock music?
murder mysteries?	jazz?
music videos?	opera?

 2 ▶ **Listen to the conversations. Does the second speaker respond *tactfully* or *tactlessly*? Check (√) the correct column.**

TACTFULLY   TACTLESSLY

1. _____   _____
2. _____   _____
3. _____   _____
4. _____   _____
5. _____   _____

 3 ▶ **Listen to the conversation.**
   ▶ **Act out similar conversations. Your partner will suggest an activity from the box. Respond tactfully. If the activity does not appeal to you, be sure not to hurt your partner's feelings.**

A There's a new exhibit of fifteenth-century Italian paintings at the museum. Maybe we ought to go there sometime.

B That might be interesting, but modern art is what I really like.

A Oh, really? I guess I'm rather traditional. Modern art doesn't appeal to me too much.

You've heard that . . .

there's a new exhibit of fifteenth-century Italian paintings at the museum.
the Pilobolus Dance Theater is going to be at the Cultural Center for a week.
Julio Iglesias is going to perform at the Bijou Theater.
there's a terrific seven-day tour of Great Britain advertised in the newspaper.

Some tactful responses

That might be interesting, but _____ is what I really like.
Actually, I don't really care for _____ too much. _____ is what I really like.
I wouldn't mind seeing _____ , but _____ is who I actually prefer.
To tell you the truth, _____ doesn't really appeal to me. _____ is where I'd rather go.

4 ▶ **Study the frames:**
      Special word order for emphasis

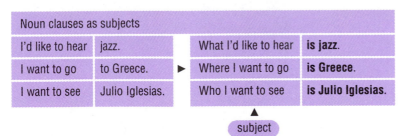

Noun clauses as subjects			
I'd like to hear	jazz.	What I'd like to hear	**is jazz.**
I want to go	to Greece.	Where I want to go	**is Greece.**
I want to see	Julio Iglesias.	Who I want to see	**is Julio Iglesias.**

subject

Noun clauses as subject complements			
I'd like to hear	jazz.	**Jazz is**	what I'd like to hear.
I want to go	to Greece.	**Greece is**	where I want to go.
I want to see	Julio Iglesias.	**Julio Iglesias is**	who I want to see.

subject complement

5 ▶ **Restate the conversation, changing the sentences in brackets [ ] to give them more emphasis. Each sentence may be restated in two different ways.**

A A new play is opening at the National Theater. It's a musical. We'll have to see it.

B That sounds good, but [I'd really like to see an opera sometime.]

A I don't know. In musicals, [you hear lively music.] Music you can remember and sing. I think opera is kind of dull.

B How do you know? You've never been to one!

A Well, that may be, but [I'd still rather go to that new musical.] The problem with opera is that you can't understand any of the words.

B [You need a translation.]

A Well, maybe, but . . .

B Listen, I can't stand the fact that we never do anything different. Maybe *we're* dull.

A Well, O.K. But if I have to go, [I'd really like to hear Placido Domingo.]

A *A new play . . .*

B *That sounds good, but what I'd really like to see sometime is an opera.* or
That sounds good, but an opera is what I'd really like to see sometime.

 6 ▶ **Listen to the conversation.**
   ▶ **Act out similar conversations with a partner. You are enthusiastic about modern things, but your partner is more conservative. Respond tactfully to his or her opinions.**

A Would you ever consider getting a tattoo?

B Me? Never. There's nothing wrong with innovative styles, yet I'm personally more comfortable with a conservative look.

A Well, you might like it once you get used to it. I wasn't sure about it myself at first, but now I think it's a great look.

Some questions
Would you ever consider getting a tattoo?
What do you think of ultramodern architecture?
Isn't abstract painting just great?
Why don't we take a Thai cooking class?

Some opinions
You like conservative styles.
You think Notre Dame is the most beautiful building in the world.
You think Renaissance painting is much more appealing.
You prefer other styles of cooking.

Some tactful responses
You might like it once you get used to it.
I wasn't sure about it myself at first, but now I think it's a great look.
Try it, you'll like it.
It's not for everyone.
It's not your cup of tea, I guess.
It takes time getting used to.

7 ▶ **Listen to the conversation.**

▶ **Act out similar conversations with a partner. You don't agree with the opinions in the box. Discuss your reactions to these people's blunt remarks with your partner.**

A I love opera, whereas / while my husband can't stand it.

He said he'd rather listen to a cat fight.

B How did you react when he said that?

A Well, I just laughed it off. People have a right to their opinions.

B Nevertheless, / Nonetheless, I think they should be more open-minded.

Some opinions
Your husband said he'd rather listen to a cat fight than an opera.
Your wife says she can't stand abstract painting. She thinks any five year old could do better.
Your friend thinks modern architecture is horrible. He/She said new buildings all look like cereal boxes.

Some reactions to blunt remarks
I found it offensive/rude.
I considered it an insult/insulting.
I found it amusing.
I just laughed it off.

8 ▶ **Study the frames: Connectors *in spite of* and *despite; yet; nevertheless* and *nonetheless; whereas* and *while;* and *however* and *on the other hand***

I really didn't like that movie	**in spite of** **despite**	the good reviews.	
The acting was excellent,	**yet**	I was still disappointed.	
I wouldn't recommend the movie.	**Nevertheless,** **Nonetheless,**	I'm not sorry I went.	
The heroine was perfect for her role,	**whereas** **while**	the hero was completely miscast.	
The acting was excellent.	The subject,	**however,** **on the other hand,**	was boring.

9 ▶ **Christie, an American teenager, is visiting relatives in Germany during her summer vacation. Rewrite her letter to her parents, completing the sentences with appropriate connectors from exercise 8. All items but one have two answers.**

July 23

Dear Mom and Dad,

   Wait till I tell you where I've been. You know how Uncle Karl and Aunt Marlene love opera, _____ I have never been able to stand it. Well, they decided to take me to the Wagner Festival in Bayreuth! I really didn't want to go, _____ I didn't want to say anything to hurt their feelings. I wasn't looking forward to sitting through days and days of opera. _____ , I actually enjoyed the whole trip.

   The city is full of fantastic eighteenth-century buildings, and the festival theater is beautiful. The singers were really good and some of the music wasn't bad, either. The operas, _____ , were too long for me. I don't think I'd want to go again _____ the good time I had. I'll take a rock concert any day!

   All our relatives here send you their love. I miss you both a lot _____ the fact that I'm having such a great time.

Love,
Christie

59. Your turn

1. Look at the posters advertising the different events, and look at the pictures of the people and the information about them. Then, working in groups, discuss these questions.

   1. Which event would each of these people probably prefer to attend the most? Why?
   2. Suppose each of these people asked your group to go to the event with him or her. Which events would you want to go to and why? Which ones would you not want to go to and why not?

2. Work with a partner and discuss the event or events you would never go to. What would you say if someone invited you to one of them?

🔊 Listen in

Bart is talking to a friend about one of the events in the posters. Listen to the conversation and then say which event Bart is talking about.

Great Rivers of the World
LECTURE

Thursday, October 9, 8:00 P.M.
Public Library, Main Branch

**Illustrated with color slides
from five continents**

Ancient Instruments

*An Exhibition at the
University School of Music*

Including instruments from the Roman Empire through medieval times. On display will be a sistrum, a lyre, a viola da gamba, a cithara, a harpsichord, and many more.

Starts Tuesday,
Noon to 7:00 P.M.

Rosa is a retired legal secretary who spends her time playing music on a variety of instruments. She composes the music herself.

Martin is a scholar who is interested in geography and history and would like to be a professor someday.

MIDNIGHT MUSICAL CRUISE

Live Dixieland Jazz Band

Departs from Seaside Wharf for a cruise of the upper and lower bay
Breakfast provided at sunrise

Saturday night, October 11
Call 555-4198 for reservations.

Rock Opera
LIVE PERFORMANCE OF A NEW ROCK OPERA

Featuring Local Performers

Municipal Auditorium
People in costume
admitted free

Oct. 10–17, 8:00 P.M.
No advance reservations.
Tickets on sale
from 6:00 P.M. on

FILM PREVIEW
NEW DOCUMENTARY ON THE SPANISH CIVIL WAR

Featuring rare film clips and stills
Sponsored by the Discovery History Club
Soundtrack features Spanish folk songs of the era

Tuesday night, October 7 • One performance only

Call 555-8062
Tickets are limited.

Janice works very hard at an import-export business. What little spare time she has she likes to spend fishing. She also likes to dance.

Juan is a photographer who has traveled around the world on assignments. He also has a large collection of historical photographs.

60. On your own

1. **Answer the letter. Respond tactfully as you tell your friends your preferences.**

Dear _____,

It was great talking to you on the phone the other evening. We're really happy you can spend the weekend with us. We plan to have a lot of fun—just like we used to have when we all lived in the same city. Here are some of the things we think you might be interested in doing with us:

• Attend the Classic Film Festival sponsored by the Film Club at our local community college. We can see four films in one day!

• Watch the annual Kitty Beauty Pageant at the downtown mall. They give prizes to the best groomed and most originally dressed cats.

• Go camping in Moorland Forest, about twenty miles north of us. Although it might get a little cold at night, we can build a nice big fire and take warm clothes with us.

• Watch the annual fireworks display as we listen to the city band play. That's in Central Park. We can take a picnic supper and sit on a blanket and eat as we enjoy the show.

• Stay home one night so you can watch the slides of our vacation to Lazy Lake. We must have taken a hundred of them!

How's that sound to you? Write and let us know your preferences.

See you soon,

Sally & Chris

2. **Sometimes we accept invitations to do things or to go places, just to be polite, so we don't hurt other people's feelings. Write about an experience you didn't enjoy, but which you felt obligated to participate in.**

Review of units 7–12

1 ► As you read the article, pay attention to the differences between Brazilian and North American students in their attitudes toward time. Then, based on the information in the article, decide whether the speaker in each of these items is Brazilian or North American.

1. "I'd like to help you, but I can't or I'll be late for class."

2. "I can probably meet you around 1:00. It depends on what time my class ends today."

3. "I don't think Marisa will have much success as a lawyer. She's never on time for anything."

4. "I'm supposed to be at Sylvia's for dinner in five minutes. I guess I'd better start getting dressed."

5. "Marvin used to always keep me waiting—in front of the theater or restaurant, or wherever we went—so I stopped going out with him."

SOCIAL TIME: The Heartbeat of Culture

BY ROBERT LEVINE WITH ELLEN WOLFF

"If a man does not keep pace with his companions, perhaps it is because he hears a different drummer." This thought by Thoreau strikes a chord in so many people that it has become part of our language. We use the phrase "the beat of a different drummer" to explain any pace of life unlike our own. Such colorful vagueness reveals how informal our rules of time really are. The world over, children simply "pick up" their society's time concepts as they mature. No dictionary clearly defines the meaning of "early" or "late" for them or for strangers who stumble over the maddening differences between the time sense they bring with them and the one they face in a new land.

I learned this firsthand, a few years ago, when I accepted an appointment as visiting professor of psychology at the federal university in Niterói, Brazil. On my first day of class I arrived to find an empty room. The class was scheduled from 10:00 until noon. Many students came late, some very late. Several arrived after 10:30. A few showed up closer to 11:00. Two came after that. All of the latecomers wore the relaxed smiles that I came, later, to enjoy. Each one said hello, and although a few apologized briefly, none seemed terribly concerned about lateness. They assumed that I understood.

The real surprise, however, came at noon that first day, when the end of class arrived. Back home in California, I never need to look at a clock to know when the class hour is ending. The shuffling of books is accompanied by strained expressions that say plaintively, "I'm going to die if you keep us one more second." When noon arrived in my first Brazilian class, only a few students left immediately. Others slowly drifted out during the next 15 minutes, and some continued asking me questions long after that.

Are Brazilians simply more flexible in their concepts of time and punctuality? With the assistance of colleagues Laurie West and Harry Reis, I compared the time sense of 91 male and female students in Niterói with that of 107 similar students at California State University in Fresno. When we asked students to give typical reasons for lateness, the Brazilians were less likely to say it was caused by not caring than the North Americans were. Instead, they pointed to unpredictable events that the person couldn't control. Because they seemed less likely to feel personally responsible for being late, they also expressed less regret for their own lateness and blamed others less when they were late.

We found similar differences in how students from the two countries talked about people who were late for appointments. Unlike their North American counterparts, the Brazilian students believed that a person who is consistently late is probably more successful than one who is consistently on time. They seemed to accept the idea that someone of importance is expected to arrive late, and they saw lack of punctuality as a sign of success.

Formal "clock time" may be a standard on which the world agrees, but "social time," the heartbeat of culture, is something else again. How a country paces its social life is a mystery to most outsiders. When we realize we are out of step, we often blame the people around us to make ourselves feel better.

Appreciating cultural differences in people's sense of time becomes increasingly important as modern technology puts more and more people in daily contact. If we are to avoid misunderstandings that involve time perceptions, we need to understand better our own cultural biases and those of others.

2 ▶ Rewrite the paragraphs, completing the sentences with one of the connectors in the box. Some items have two answers.

despite
however
in spite of
nevertheless
nonetheless
on the other hand
whereas
while
yet

_____ the fact that both Brazilians and North Americans use the standard twelve-hour clock, they have a very different sense of social time. Both Brazilian and North American university students have fixed class schedules, _____ the words "early" and "late" do not have the same meaning in both countries. For example, Brazilian students are casual about arriving exactly on time for class, _____ North American students are very punctual. North Americans see being late for appointments as a sign of a disorganized, unsuccessful person. Brazilians, _____, are likely to consider being late a sign of a busy, successful person.

Robert Levine, the author of an article on social time, was surprised at first by his students' lateness; _____ , he later came to appreciate their relaxed attitudes. Understanding cultural differences makes it possible for people to understand each other and work together _____ cultural biases.

3 ▶ John gives Mike a ride to class every morning, but Mike is always late. Restate their conversation, combining the sentences in brackets [ ] into one sentence that contains an infinitive or gerund with a subject.

John Come on, Mike. [You're late every morning. I'm tired of it.]
Come on, Mike. I'm tired of your being late every morning.

Mike I wish you wouldn't keep telling me that. [People always nag me. I don't like it.]

John Well, [you keep me waiting every day. I don't like that.]

Mike I know, but [people hurry me so much. I'm not used to it.] And [classes start right on time. I'm not accustomed to that,] either.

John I realize that. And [you're getting mad at me. I don't want that,] but we really have to be on time for class here.

4 ▶ Comment on each of the situations below, starting your sentences with _By then_ . . . or _By the time_ . . . and using the clues in parentheses. Use a future perfect or future perfect continuous form of each verb.

1. Your aunt, who is going overseas for three years, won't be able to see your new apartment before she leaves. (I/live/for three years)
By the time my aunt sees my new apartment, I will have been living in it for three years.

2. You're going to a lecture from 8:00 to 9:30. Your friend Tony wants to go but he has a class until 8:30. (he/miss/more than a half hour)

3. You and your friends are taking part in a clean-up day in your neighborhood from noon until 6:00 P.M. Your friend Susana can't make it until 4:00. (we/work/for four hours)

4. There are two soccer games on Saturday, the first one at 1:00 and the second one at 3:00. You're going to both games, but your friend Hector doesn't get off work until 2:30. (the first game/end)

5 ► As you read the story, think ahead to how it might end. When you have finished reading, give your interpretations of Todd's decision, considering these questions.

1. What kind of person do you think Todd is?
2. What problems does Todd have?
3. Is the ending surprising? Why or why not?
4. Are there any lines earlier in the story that give a clue to the ending?

6 ► Now write your own ending to the story. When you have finished, share it with a group of classmates. Talk about Todd's motives and decide which of the different possible endings seems most likely. You may wish to use the expressions in the box.

He must have (been) . . .
He couldn't have (been) . . .
He wouldn't have (been) . . .
Despite . . .
Therefore . . .
And so . . .
If he . . . , then . . .
. . . , which seems strange.
What convinces me that . . . is
  when he says . . .

Night Shift

by Gloria Rosenthal

Todd blew on his fingers as he ran back to the comforting shelter of the gas station office. The car he had just serviced pulled away in a smoke screen of warm air hitting the cold night. Todd was alone.

Three A.M., he thought. Four more hours before Jess would be in to take over. He closed his eyes and listened to the voices coming at him from a beat-up radio. "Wait a minute. Hold it a minute," Todd heard the announcer's voice say. "I've got a news flash, folks." The announcer cleared his throat and changed his tone of voice. "The Country National Bank of Long Island was broken into tonight. Two armed men killed the night guard and a police officer who responded to the alarm. A second police officer was critically injured, but not before he fatally wounded one of the men. The other man got away and was possibly heading for the Southern State Parkway."

Todd stood up and walked around the small office trying to see out into the cold night, but all he could see were his own station lights throwing out a dim circle of light. He couldn't see the Southern State Parkway. But he knew it was out there.

The next news flash came about 20 minutes later. The gunman had abandoned his car on the side of the highway just after Exit 19 in Hempstead. The police did not know how he was traveling but thought that he might have been picked up by another motorist.

"Hey," the talk-show host added, "with his hundred and fifty grand, he could have taken a cab."

Todd whistled, "One hundred and fifty thousand!" Here's this guy who just walks into a bank and helps himself to $150,000. Todd thought of the trouble he and Jess had raising the money for the gas station. So many small loans from family and friends. So many papers to sign. So much money to pay back.

When a horn—sounding too loud in the still night—broke into his thoughts, Todd jumped. He didn't realize how nervous he had become. Even more surprising was finding his hand reaching into the desk drawer. When he finally found the gun beneath some papers, it felt cold in his hand, maybe because his hand had suddenly begun to sweat. He put the gun in his pocket.

He heard, rather than saw, the car door open. Then he saw a short woman in a ski jacket running toward him, "Ladies' room?" she questioned. Todd smiled, a flood of relief actually warming him.

Another news flash: The armed robber had gotten a ride along Sunrise Highway and somewhere near Wantagh Parkway had pushed out the driver. So now they knew the gunman was in a white Cutlass with a red roof. License plate number LJR1939.

"I'm glad I'm in this nice safe studio," came the voice of the announcer. "Watch out, out there. Be careful of white cars. Don't pick up any strangers. And all you guys in gas stations better not service a white Cutlass with a red roof."

Todd saw the headlights coming at him as the car swung into the station and pulled up slowly at the pump. There it was. A white car with a red roof. He saw the license number in the pale light. LJR1939.

What should he do? Todd had to make a quick decision.

"Yes, sir?"

"Fill 'er up—premium," the man said, sounding like a hundred other motorists on a hundred other nights.

The tank was full, and as he replaced the hose, Todd kept his eye on the man.

"Check your oil, sir?" Todd asked while making up his mind for sure. He had to be careful.

"No, thanks," was all the man said, but it was all the time Todd needed. He had the gun in his hand and at the man's head in one smooth motion.

"Freeze!" Todd said, and the man froze. "Keep one hand on the wheel and hand me that briefcase."

7 ▶ **Rewrite the paragraph about the robbery, combining each pair of sentences in brackets [ ] into one sentence using *either . . . or*, *neither . . . nor*, or *not only . . . but (also).***

Police are completely confused over the robbery at the Country National Bank of Long Island. [They haven't found the robber. What's more, they don't have a clue to his whereabouts.] [The robber must have found a very secure hiding place. If not, then he's vanished into thin air.] After stealing a white Cutlass with a red roof and a nearly empty gas tank, [the robber would have had to get gas. If not, he would have had to find another car.] However, [the police have not found the Cutlass, and they have not received any reports of other stolen cars.] Kevin Daly, the owner of the stolen car, said that [the robber didn't look suspicious, and he didn't seem nervous.] While police are without a clue, they won't give up easily on this crime. [The robber stole $150,000 from the bank. What's more, he killed one police officer and critically injured another.]

8 ▶ **Here is one possible explanation of what happens to the money. Read the statements below. Then listen to the conversation between Todd and Jess, and choose *a* or *b*.**

1. Todd decided to _____ .
   a. keep the money
   b. give the money back

2. Jess thinks Todd should have _____ .
   a. kept the money
   b. given the money back

3. Todd is probably _____ honest than Jess.
   a. more
   b. less

4. Jess probably _____ if his kids led a life of crime.
   a. wouldn't care
   b. would be upset

9 ▶ **It is now several days after the robbery. What are the different people thinking now? Complete each statement with the correct form of the verbs in parentheses.**

1. Todd: If I *weren't* (not be) always so honest, I *would have kept* (keep) that $150,000 instead of giving it back to the police.

2. Jess: If Todd _____ (not give back) that money, our troubles _____ (be) over."

3. Jess: If Todd and I really _____ (like) working at the gas station, I _____ (not feel) this way.

4. Night guard's widow: If he _____ (retire) last month like he said he was going to, he _____ (be) alive today.

5. Police captain: They were good cops, but if they _____ (be) a little more careful, Jack _____ (be) alive and Bill _____ (not have) a bullet in his chest.

6. Wounded police officer: If I _____ (not kill) that one guy, I _____ (be) dead now.

7. Radio announcer: If that guy _____ (not be) so dumb, he _____ (not steal) a car without any gas in it.

10 ▶ **As you read the article, look for answers to the questions below. When you have finished reading, answer the questions briefly.**

1. How have the eating habits of people in the United States changed over the past several years?

2. What are four reasons for the change?

ETHNIC EATERIES ADD SPICE TO DINING

BY JOHN MARIANI

Former meat-and-potatoes eaters, people across the United States are developing a great appetite for foods they had never heard of.

They are ordering Greek *taramosalata* made of mashed cod roe and olive oil and Japanese sea urchins with green *wasabi* horseradish. They can grasp slippery snow peas with chopsticks, digest red-hot Indian curries, and expertly twirl strands of fettuccine on their forks.

In response, restaurants are serving more authentic ethnic foods. For example, Chinese restaurants are replacing chow mein and egg rolls with shark's fin soup, sea cucumber, and sweet bean-paste buns.

The reasons for this enormous enthusiasm for ethnic food: increased interest in authentic dishes, more dining out, the impact of immigrants, an emphasis on nutrition, and improved trade.

Working men and women who have traveled abroad and who have the money are dining out more often. The restaurant industry is trying hard to appeal to this group.

"People want things made correctly, authentically, and the way they remember them from their travels abroad," says *Food and Wine* magazine columnist Stanley Dry.

Ethnic groups new to the United States have brought their cuisines with them. Immigrant Hoang Ming, who opened one of the first Vietnamese restaurants in Washington, D.C., says that most of the authentic Asian restaurants in Washington have opened in the last few years, primarily in low-rent districts.

Ming admits that the food at his first restaurants, although authentic, was adapted for American tastes. He feels that customers have become more educated. "Now I can serve exotic dishes and know my clientele will love them. They're fascinated."

The popularity of fresh, exotic foods is also due to a demand by diners for healthier, less-fatty foods. Says Chicago cardiologist Dr. Anthony Chan: "The [Asian] diet is not centered on red meat, and they use almost no butter, milk, cream, or cheese. It contains about half the fat of the American diet, and the Chinese eat small portions of non-fatty meats and fish and a lot of fiber like rice."

Most authentic ethnic foods are based on small portions, fresh seasonal vegetables, and quick cooking. True Italian food is not heavily layered with sauces and cheese, but depends on cholesterol-free olive oil, lots of vegetables, and grilled fish.

Asian stir-frying and steaming techniques retain nutrients far better than deep frying or boiling. Mexican food is high in carbohydrates such as beans and rice, and Japanese food centers on fish.

Heavier ethnic cuisines—such as German, Polish, and Hungarian, all high in fat and cholesterol—have not shown any increased popularity.

More than anything else, interest in ethnic cuisines has grown because increased trade has brought in many foods and ingredients never before seen in the United States. One delicacy shop in New York carries 40 different kinds of olive oil and 300 cheeses, as well as a wide array of other foods that couldn't be found at any price ten years ago.

11 ▶ **Rewrite the paragraphs below about a new restaurant, changing the sentences in brackets [ ] into sentences containing double comparatives.**

Mama Rosa's Authentic Italian Pizzeria doesn't live up to its name. My family and I visited Mama Rosa's several times in the last two weeks, and [each time we ate there, we liked it less.] My children tried to improve the taste of the pizza by adding cheese. But [when they added more cheese, it only got worse.] [Each time I think about it, I become more convinced that the pizza is prepared in advance and then frozen.]

Mama Rosa's pizza is neither authentic nor Italian. [The place should close as soon as possible, and we'll be better off.]

Start like this:
. . . *My family and I visited Mama Rosa's several times in the last two weeks, and the more we ate there, the less we liked it.*

12 ▶ Restate the conversations, changing the sentences in brackets [ ] to give them more emphasis. Each sentence may be restated in two different ways.

1. **A** These rolls from Stella's Bakery are pretty good.
   B They're not bad, but [I'd rather have a real French croissant.]
   A *These rolls from Stella's Bakery are pretty good.*
   B *They're not too bad, but what I'd rather have is a real French croissant.* or
   They're not too bad, but a real French croissant is what I'd rather have.

2. **A** I'd like dessert, but I don't want anything fattening.
   B I can't help you there. [I always order one of those delicious, rich pastries.]

3. **A** There aren't very many Japanese restaurants in this city.
   B I've noticed that. [I'd like to find a Japanese grocery store around here, too.]

4. **A** Are you sure I can't convince you to have another piece of coconut cream pie?
   B No, thanks. When it comes to my diet, [I have to listen to my doctor.]

5. **A** When I was in Mexico, I was surprised at what real Mexican food is like. It's so different from the Mexican food in restaurants here.
   B I know what you mean. When I was in Italy, [real Italian pizza surprised me.]

13 ▶ Using the information in the article, add more information to each of these sentences by including a nonrestrictive relative clause.

1. I really like a chili seasoning called *berbere.*
   I really like a chili seasoning called berbere, *which is used in Ethiopian cooking.*
2. Vietnamese food uses a fish sauce of fermented anchovies.
3. Korean dishes often have hot seasoning.
4. Southern Italian cuisine features dry pasta and seafood.
5. Cooks in northern Italy roast or braise lamb and veal, and grill fish.
6. The main seasonings in Thai food include coriander and garlic.
7. The Moroccan dish called *couscous* is made from steamed millet grain.

THE FLAVORS OF INTERNATIONAL FOODS
Here are some basic differences in ethnic foods:

KOREAN Similar to Chinese and specializing in barbecuing and noodle dishes, often with hot seasoning.

THAI Maybe the hottest food in the world, with plenty of chili peppers. Main seasonings include coriander, garlic, tamarind, lemon grass, and coconut milk.

VIETNAMESE Fragant, with a colonial link to French food. This is not highly peppered food; the predominant flavoring is a fish sauce of fermented anchovies.

ETHIOPIAN Based on stewed meats and vegetables and eaten on a thin pancake called injera. It can be extremely hot when berbere, a chili seasoning, is added.

MOROCCAN A rich, diverse cookery whose national dish is couscous, made from steamed millet grain topped with chicken, lamb, and other meats. There is often a sweet-salty balance.

NORTHERN ITALIAN Specializes in fresh pasta, vegetables, cream sauces, mushrooms, and cornmeal polenta. Lamb and veal are roasted or braised, and fish is grilled.

SOUTHERN ITALIAN Lots of tomato, onion, garlic, and basil, with dry pasta and such seafood as shellfish, squid, or salted cod called baccala.

14 ▶ Nick and George, two waiters at a Greek restaurant, came to work early to help their boss open the restaurant. When they arrived, they found a note from their boss. Rewrite the note, reducing the relative clauses as in the example.

Start like this:
The tables in the back room need to be set. . . .

The tables that are in the back room need to be set. The glasses that are in the sink have to be washed and dried. The pastries that are in the kitchen have to be displayed in the dessert case. The woman who is wearing a red shirt and jeans is Jennifer, the new waitress. Give her the uniform that is in the storage closet.

THE LANGUAGE OF PERSUASION

BY DAVID KIPNIS AND STUART SCHMIDT

Rational, insistent, and emotional statements all have one thing in common. They show people trying to persuade others, a skill we all treasure. Books about power and influence are read by young executives eager for a promotion, by politicians anxious to influence the voters, by lonely people looking to win and hold a mate, and by upset parents trying to make their children see the light.

Despite this interest in persuasion, most people are not really aware of how they go about it. They spend more time choosing their clothes than choosing their influence styles. Even fewer are aware of how their styles affect others or themselves. Although shouts and demands may make people dance to our tune, we will probably lose their good will. People's opinions of us may change for the worse when we use hard or abusive tactics.

We conducted studies of dating couples and business managers in which the couples described how they attempted to influence their partners, and the managers told how they attempted to influence their subordinates, peers, and superiors at work. We then used these descriptions as the basis for separate questionnaires in which we asked other couples and managers how frequently they employed each tactic. We found that the tactics could be classified into three basic strategies—hard, soft, and rational, as shown in the charts below.

People sometimes ask,"Which tactic works best?" The answer is that they all work if they are used at the right time with the right person. But both hard and soft tactics involve costs to the user even when they succeed. Hard tactics often alienate the people being influenced and create a climate of hostility and resistance. Soft tactics—acting nice, being humble—may lessen self-respect and self-esteem. In contrast, we found that people who rely chiefly on logic, reason, and compromise to get their way are the most satisfied both with their business lives and with their personal relationships.

> **"I had all the facts and figures ready before I made my suggestions to my boss."** **(Manager)**
> —*Rational Statement*
>
> **"I kept insisting that we do it my way. She finally caved in."** **(Husband)**
> —*Insistent Statement*
>
> **"I think it's about time that you stop thinking these negative things about yourself."** **(Psychotherapist)**
> —*Rational Statement*
>
> **"Send out more horses, skirr the country round. Hang those that talk of fear. Give me mine armour."** **(Macbeth, Act 5)**
> —*Emotional Statement*

INFLUENCE STRATEGIES

Strategy	Couples	Managers
HARD	I get angry and demand that he/she give in.	I simply order the person to do what I want.
	As the first step I make him/her feel stupid and worthless.	I threaten to give an unsatisfactory performance evaluation.
	I say I'll leave him/her if my spouse does not agree.	I get higher management to back up my request.
SOFT	I act warm and charming before bringing up the subject.	I act very humble while making my request.
	I am so nice that he/she cannot refuse.	I make the person feel important by saying that she/he has the brains and experience to do what I want.
RATIONAL	I offer to compromise; I'll give up a little if he/she gives up a little.	I offer to exchange favors: You do this for me, and I'll do something for you.
	We talk, discussing our views objectively without arguments.	I explain the reason for my request.

WHY PEOPLE CHOOSE EACH STRATEGY

Hard tactics are normally used when:

Influencer has the advantage.
Resistance is anticipated.
Behavior of the other person goes against social or organizational standards.

Soft tactics are normally used when:

Influencer is at a disadvantage.
Resistance is anticipated.
The goal is to get benefits for one's self.

Rational tactics are normally used when:

Neither party has a real power advantage.
Resistance is not anticipated.
The goal is to get benefits for one's self and one's organization.

15 ▶ As you read the article on page 135, pay attention to the differences among the three basic strategies of persuasion—hard, soft, and rational. Then identify which strategy each of these speakers is using.

1. (Parent to child) Get upstairs and clean your room! Now. *Hard.*

2. (Employer to employee) I'm awfully sorry to ask you to stay late, but I know I can't solve this problem without your help.

3. (Wife to husband) If you'll do the shopping while I do the laundry, I'll be free to go to the game with you this afternoon.

4. (Employer to employee) I strongly suggest that you work this problem out. If not, I will have to write a negative report about you.

5. (Husband to wife) That was the best spaghetti I ever had. Why don't we invite my mother over on Sunday, so you can cook some for her?

6. (Employer to employee) If you can make this trip to Los Angeles over the weekend, I'll see that you get two days off next week.

16 ▶ Complete each of the conversations below by supplying an appropriate request for the first speaker.

1. **A** (Bart Conti, a bank branch manager, has lost his copy of the plan for new accounts. He asks Marlene Lundberg, the manager of another branch, to send him a copy.)
   B Sure, Bart, I'll send one right over.

   A *Marlene, I seem to have lost my copy of the plan for new accounts. Could you send me a copy?*
   B *Sure, Bart. I'll send one right over.*

2. **A** (Teresa Colon, the head teller, asks Gilbert Kohler, a teller, to find the records of the Hoffman account for her.)
   B Of course, Ms. Colon.

3. **A** (Jung Kim, a teller, asks Bart Conti if he can change his work schedule the following week, to work late on Friday instead of Tuesday.)
   B I suppose that's all right.

4. **A** (Jung Kim asks Gilbert Kohler, who was planning to work late on Friday but not on Tuesday, to change late days with him.)
   B Yeah, that's O.K., Jung.

17 ▶ Sophia is a very talented but rather lazy young piano student. Restate her music teacher's advice by changing the subjunctive clauses to infinitive clauses and the infinitive clauses to subjunctive clauses. Then decide if the music teacher's strategy is hard, soft, or rational.

"I guess there's nothing more I can say or do to persuade you to try harder, Sophia. At this point, it's crucial that *you* decide what you really want to do. In order to be a great pianist, it's important for a person to start early. You're very talented, but it's still essential that you practice on a daily basis. It's also very important for you to come to class regularly and bring your music. No one can do these things for you—and no one should. It's necessary that you decide yourself whether to make these changes in your attitude or to give up your future as a pianist."